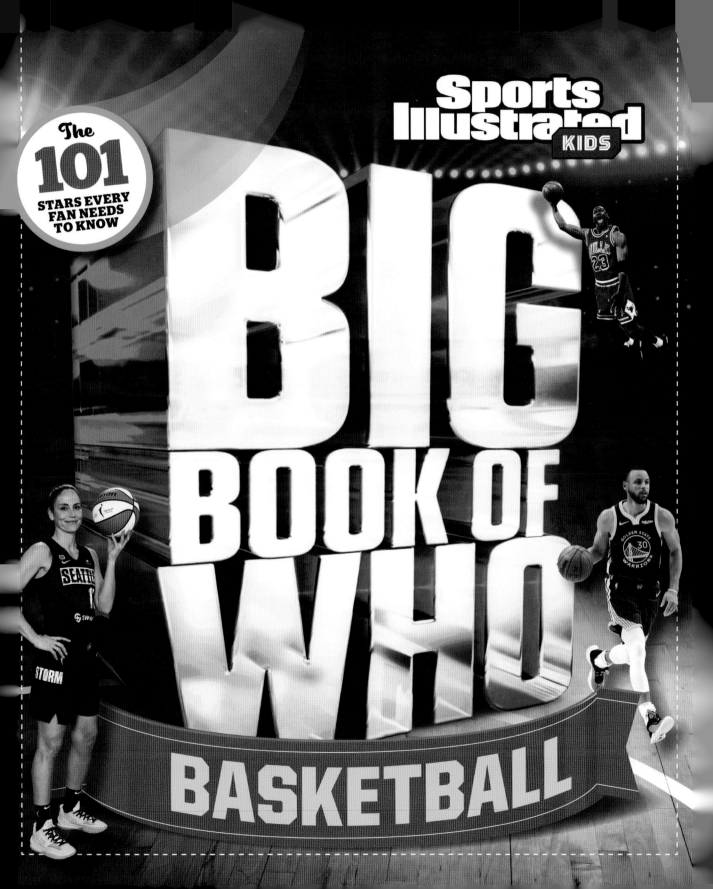

The **101** STARS EVERY FAN NEEDS TO KNOW

Sports Illustrated KIDS

BIG BOOK OF WHO

BASKETBALL

Library of Congress Cataloging-in-Publication Data available upon request.
ISBN 978-1-63727-251-0
Printed in China

This book is available in quantity at special discounts for your group or organization.

For further information, contact:
Triumph Books LLC
814 North Franklin Street
Chicago, Illinois 60610
(312) 337-0747
www.triumphbooks.com

Produced by
Shoreline Publishing Group LLC
Santa Barbara, California
Designer: Tom Carling, Carling Design Inc.

Updates to 2022 edition text
by James Buckley Jr.

WELCOME

Basketball is an exciting game filled with dunks, buzzer beaters, and thrilling plays made by the sport's biggest stars. This book features all the greats, from amazing shooters to sensational playmakers to imposing rebounders. Who was the youngest player to win the NBA MVP Award? Who has the most scoring titles in WNBA history? Find out the answers to those questions and more in this book of basketball's best players, both past and present.

CONTENTS

CHAM

These players led their teams to the ultimate prize in basketball

PIONS

FAST FACT: Parker is the Spurs' franchise leader in assists with 6,829.

SUPER STAT

2013

THE YEAR THAT PARKER LED HIS HOME COUNTRY OF FRANCE TO ITS FIRST EUROPEAN CHAMPIONSHIP

Who was the first European-born player to be named NBA Finals MVP?

When Gregg Popovich, the coach of the San Antonio Spurs, first heard about a 6´2˝ guard from France named **TONY PARKER**, he thought the same thing as most NBA executives: "Everybody knows you don't get point guards from Europe," he said, "because they're generally not quick enough and they don't have a grasp of the NBA game." But after watching film of Parker compete against promising U.S. players, Popovich was sold. The Spurs selected the 19-year-old with the 28th overall pick in the 2001 NBA Draft. Over the course of the next 18 seasons, Parker would win four NBA titles and become the first European-born player to be named NBA Finals MVP.

In the fifth game after Parker's NBA debut—which made him the third Frenchman ever to play in an NBA game as well as the youngest player ever to suit up for the Spurs—he took over as the starting point guard. Playing alongside stars Tim Duncan and David Robinson, he led his team in assists and steals and made the All-Rookie team. Parker helped San Antonio win NBA championships in 2003 and '05, but it wasn't until the 2007 Finals that Parker really stole the spotlight. He shot 56.8% from the field and averaged 24.5 points, almost six points more than his regular-season average that year, on his way to being the NBA Finals MVP in a sweep of the Cleveland Cavaliers.

Who was MVP of the first four WNBA Finals?

Guard **CYNTHIA COOPER** is one of the greatest women's basketball players of all time, but the WNBA didn't exist when the two-time NCAA national champion finished her career at the University of Southern California. So in 1986, the guard took off for Europe, where she would lead Spanish and Italian leagues in scoring nine times over the next decade. Before the WNBA's inaugural 1997 season, Cooper, at the age of 34, signed on to play for the Houston Comets. She immediately established her dominance—Cooper won four WNBA Finals MVPs while her team lost a total of only three playoff games. Cooper also led the WNBA in scoring her first three years and was named the regular season MVP her first two seasons.

FAST FACT: Bill Russell has the most championship rings in NBA history. He won 11 with the Celtics.

Who had the most rebounds in an NBA Finals game?

Boston Celtics big man **BILL RUSSELL** grabbed a record 40 rebounds in Game 2 of the 1960 Finals against the St. Louis Hawks, then matched that in a 1962 Game 7 victory over the Los Angeles Lakers. Over his 13-year NBA career, he pulled down 21,620 rebounds, averaging 22.5 per game. He led the league in total rebounds four times. Since blocked shots were not tracked during the Celtics legend's career—and because the small things, such as setting picks, basket-to-basket foot speed, and fast-break passing will always go unappreciated—rebounding may be the only stat that truly shows how dominant the five-time MVP was.

Who is the only player to win NBA Finals MVP with three different teams?

Several NBA players have been good—and lucky—enough to win NBA titles with three different teams. Only **LeBRON JAMES** has earned the NBA Finals MVP that way. He won his first in 2012 with the Miami Heat, a feat he repeated in 2013. After making a big move back to his hometown Cleveland Cavaliers, he got his third NBA Finals MVP on team No. 2 in 2016. The player many think is the NBA's all-time best moved to the Los Angeles Lakers in 2018. In 2020, he was the NBA Finals MVP for a fourth time: team No. 3!

SUPER STAT

1,562

THROUGH 2022, THE NUMBER OF POINTS SCORED BY JAMES IN NBA FINALS GAMES, SECOND-MOST ALL TIME BEHIND ONLY JERRY WEST

FAST FACT: In 2000, O'Neal was named MVP of the All-Star Game, the NBA FInals, and the regular season. He became the third player, after Willis Reed and Michael Jordan, to take home all three honors in the same season.

Who is the last player to win three straight NBA Finals MVPs?

Dominant center **SHAQUILLE O'NEAL** didn't need much time to show that he was one of the greatest big men in the game. The No. 1 pick of the 1992 NBA Draft, he won Rookie of the Year with the Orlando Magic and led the team to the Finals in 1995. He joined the Los Angeles Lakers in 1996, but the team failed to reach the NBA Finals in any of O'Neal's first three seasons there. That's when L.A. brought in legendary coach Phil Jackson.

Jackson told the 7′1″ Shaq there was no reason he couldn't become an MVP if he worked hard enough, and in 1999–2000, he did exactly that. The Lakers beat the Indiana Pacers in a Finals in which O'Neal was the leading scorer in all six games, making him an easy pick for NBA Finals MVP. The following year, the Lakers swept all three playoff series in the Western Conference and lost only one Finals game to the Philadelphia 76ers on their way to earning their second straight title. O'Neal averaged 33 points, 15.8 rebounds, 4.8 assists, and 3.4 blocks to earn his second NBA Finals MVP award. Another dominating job in 2002—this time, a four-game sweep of the New Jersey Nets—gave L.A. its three-peat and Shaq a third NBA Finals MVP.

Who was the first teenager to be the No. 1 overall pick in a WNBA Draft?

Australia's **LAUREN JACKSON**'s parents were both basketball stars who played for their national teams. (Her mother also set scoring and rebounding records at LSU.) So it's no surprise that Jackson quickly became a star on the court, as well as the first teenager to be taken with the No. 1 overall pick in the WNBA 2001 WNBA Draft.

As a 16-year-old with excellent shooting range, post play, and ball control, Jackson was the youngest player ever on Australia's national team. She helped her country win a bronze medal at the 1998 World Championships and a silver at the 2000 Olympics, where the 6´5˝ phenom led the team in points and rebounds. In 2001, she joined the Seattle Storm as the No. 1 pick. Jackson went on to play 12 seasons with the Storm, winning three WNBA MVP awards and leading Seattle to two championships.

Who starred for the first team from Canada to win an NBA title?

The Toronto Raptors joined the NBA in 1995, but didn't reach the NBA Finals until 2019. They won their only NBA title—so far—by beating Stephen Curry and the Golden State Warriors. A big reason for Toronto's success that year was the arrival, for just that one season, of **KAWHI LEONARD**. Leonard had made his name as a defensive star, twice earning the league's top honor for defense. He also had championship experience. In 2014, he was the NBA Finals MVP as the San Antonio Spurs won their fifth NBA championship. Leonard arrived to a Toronto team that had made the playoffs five years in a row, but had not been able to advance to the NBA Finals. The Raptors boasted guard Kyle Lowry, solid big men in Pascal Siakam and Serge Ibaka, and a strong bench. But they lacked that superstar power that Leonard provided. He had one of his best overall seasons, averaging 26.6 points and 7.3 rebounds per game, while once again playing great defense. He earned his second NBA Finals MVP after a six-game series.

SUPER STAT

25.8

LEONARD'S PLAYER EFFICIENCY RATING IN 2018–19, WHICH SET A TORONTO TEAM RECORD

Who has the most playoff double-doubles in NBA history?

On June 12, 2014—the same night he broke Kareem Abdul-Jabbar's record for most playoff minutes played— **TIM DUNCAN** scored 10 points and pulled down 11 rebounds to help the San Antonio Spurs defeat the Miami Heat in Game 4 of the NBA Finals. It wasn't the flashiest stat line of his career, but it was enough for the power forward to earn a record-breaking 158th playoff double-double. That's almost two full extra seasons' worth of everyday scoring and rebounding consistency, which earned Duncan the equally non-flashy nickname the Big Fundamental.

Duncan had a calm, businesslike demeanor since his college days at Wake Forest University, where he was a two-time All-American and the college player of the year in 1997. The No. 1 pick of the 1997 NBA Draft, Duncan went on to win Rookie of the Year and make the first of 15 All-Star Games. Duncan said that one reason he didn't show any emotion is because displaying frustration or disappointment would have given his opponents an advantage. Perhaps the only thing he was better known for than consistency was the dominance that came from it. Duncan collected the NBA Finals MVP award three of the five times the Spurs won the title, and was only two blocks away from earning a quadruple-double in the clinching Game 6 of the 2003 NBA Finals. When told how close he was to achieving that feat, which has occurred only four times in NBA history, he simply responded, "That's cool."

FAST FACT: Growing up in the U.S. Virgin Islands, Duncan was an elite swimmer. He stopped competing after Hurricane Hugo destroyed his team's pool in 1989.

Who scored the most points in one quarter of an NBA Finals game?

In 1988, the Detroit Pistons were up three games to two against the Los Angeles Lakers in the NBA Finals, but found themselves down 56–48 in the third quarter of Game 6. That's when guard **ISIAH THOMAS** took over, scoring the next 14 points. All of a sudden, on a fast break, Thomas crumpled to the ground with a sprained ankle. Thomas was hurt, but with the Lakers resurging, he hobbled off the bench and added another 11 points, setting a Finals record with 25 for the quarter. That gave Detroit the lead going into the fourth. Thomas finished with 43 points, six steals, a poked eye, a jammed finger, and the sprained ankle. The one shot he couldn't make was a the big one in the final minute, as the Pistons would lose both that game and the series.

FAST FACT: Mikan was so dominant that the NBA had to make rule changes, such as adding a shot clock.

Who was the first NBA player enshrined in the Hall of Fame?

Six-foot-ten **GEORGE MIKAN** was the first game-changing big man in the NBA. When the league formed in 1949, it took teams from the NBL and BAA, both of which Mikan had dominated for three seasons. (He led his teams to the 1948 NBL and 1949 BAA titles.) Mikan's Minneapolis Lakers would win the first NBA title in 1950, anchored by his average of 31.3 points in the playoffs. He won three more championships over the course of his short six-season career in the NBA. When the Hall of Fame inducted its first class in 1959, Mikan was an obvious choice.

Who is the only person to win MVP and Coach of the Year in the NBA?

Before he was regarded as one of the best shooting forwards ever, and before he had demonstrated enough wisdom to lead a team from the sidelines as a coach, **LARRY BIRD** drove a garbage truck. It was one of many community jobs the Indiana native took on after leaving college due to homesickness. He gave school another chance a year later, and after he was drafted by the Boston Celtics in 1978, Bird quickly became an all-time great. In his 13-year career, he was named NBA MVP three times and won three championship rings. The 12-time All-Star retired in 1992 and swore coaching wasn't for him, but in 1997 a job opening with his hometown Indiana Pacers proved too tempting to resist. In 1998, he won Coach of the Year as his Pacers improved by 19 wins from the previous season. As the Pacers' President of Basketball Operations, Bird was named Executive of the Year in 2012. He is the only person to win awards in so many areas of the game.

SUPER STAT

3

CONSECUTIVE MVP AWARDS WON BY BIRD (1983–84, '84–85, '85–86); HE WAS ONLY OF ONLY THREE PLAYERS TO DO SO

Who helped lead Chicago to its first WNBA championship?

The most exciting champions are often the most unexpected. When the Chicago Sky finished the 2021 WNBA season, they barely made the playoffs with a .500 record of 16–16. That record was good enough for second in the Eastern Conference, but it did not look like a record that would stand up to playoff pressure. Led by stars Kahleah Cooper and Courtney Vandersloot, the Sky knocked off the Dallas Wings in a one-game playoff. Then they faced the four-time WNBA champion Minnesota Lynx. To most fans' surprise, the Sky won 89–76 on Minnesota's home court. The Cinderella team just kept putting on new slippers. A big reason was the play of WNBA great **CANDACE PARKER**. A former WNBA MVP and Defensive Player of the Year with the Los Angeles Sparks, she had joined the Sky in a return to the area where she had grown up. Next up was the Connecticut Sun, who had the league's best record. The Sky did it again, beating the Sun in four games. Cooper led all players in scoring, while Vandersloot's 41 assists in the series were more than twice as many as any other player! The Sky faced the powerful Phoenix Mercury, with superstars Brittney Griner and Diana Taurasi. Vandersloot was a magician again, dishing out an incredible 50 assists in four games. Allie Quigley led the Sky in scoring, with Cooper right behind. In the fourth quarter of the clinching Game 4, Chicago outscored Phoenix 26–11 to secure its first WNBA title.

FAST FACT: To honor the star who grew up about 30 miles west of Chicago in Naperville. Chicago declared September 16, 2021, as "Candace Parker Day."

SUPER STAT

6

NUMBER OF GAMES THAT OLAJUWON HAD A FIVE-BY-FIVE (A GAME WITH FIVE POINTS, REBOUNDS, ASSISTS, STEALS, AND BLOCKS)

Who was the first player to win MVP, Finals MVP, and DPOY in the same season?

Growing up in Nigeria, **HAKEEM OLAJUWON** played handball and soccer and didn't pick up a basketball until he was a teenager. But he proved to be a natural in the sport. Agile and nearly seven feet tall when the Houston Rockets drafted him in 1984, Olajuwon became famous for his moves and shakes, as he incorporated head fakes and fleet footwork. No season showcased his talents better than 1993–94, when he won the league MVP and the Defensive Player of the Year awards. In a critical Game 6 against the New York Knicks in the NBA Finals, Hakeem the Dream blocked a potential game-winning three-pointer as the clock ran out. Then in Game 7, he scored a game-high 25 points to go along with 10 rebounds as Houston won its first-ever title. Olajuwon was named NBA Finals MVP and was the first player to win those three major awards in the same season.

Who was the 2020 WNBA Finals MVP?

In **BREANNA STEWART**'s fourth season with the Seattle Storm, she helped the team win its fourth WNBA championship. By leading all scorers in the 3–0 WNBA Finals sweep over the Las Vegas Aces, Stewart was an easy choice for the WNBA Finals MVP. It was another trophy in a very crowded case for Stewart, who was named the Most Outstanding Player in the NCAA Final Four a record four times. She was also the 2018 WNBA MVP and in 2016 was named the WNBA Rookie of the Year.

Who had a triple-double for the Lakers in an NBA Finals Game 7 win?

Expectations were high when the Los Angeles Lakers drafted **JAMES WORTHY** with the first pick in 1982. After all, he had been an All-American at North Carolina, winning the Most Outstanding Player at the 1982 NCAA tournament following a 28-point performance in the title game. The Lakers would win championships in 1985 and '87 with help from Worthy's playoff average of more than 20 points per game, but it was in the 1988 Finals against the Detroit Pistons in which his biggest contribution came. In a tight Game 7 victory, Worthy had 36 points, 16 rebounds, and 10 assists for only the second triple-double ever in an NBA Finals Game 7. Worthy would earn the NBA Finals MVP and become known as Big Game James.

Who has the highest scoring average in NBA playoff history?

The NBA GOAT, **MICHAEL JORDAN**, didn't make his high school varsity basketball team his sophomore year. While that's a shock, it is also one reason he became so dominant. As Jordan said during his 2009 Hall of Fame speech, not making that team turned him into a focused competitor with something to prove. In the 1985–86 season, Jordan's second year in the NBA, he led his Chicago Bulls to a playoff matchup against the Boston Celtics, which had lost only one home game all season. In Game 2, Jordan lit them up for 63 points, the most ever in a playoff game. Two years later, Jordan put up back-to-back 50-point games as the Bulls beat the Cleveland Cavaliers. With his team trailing early in Game 1 of the 1992 Finals, Jordan scored 33 points in 17 minutes and broke the playoff record for three-point baskets in a single half. In the 1993 Finals, he averaged a Finals-record 41 points per game. Add it all up, and Jordan's playoff-record scoring average (33.4 points) is higher than his regular-season-record scoring average (30.1).

Who is the four-time WNBA champ that led the U.S. to a record five Olympic gold medals?

The NBA has the legendary Larry Bird. The WNBA has the incredible **SUE BIRD**. It's hard to choose which one flew higher in their sport. By any measure, Sue Bird is one of the greatest players ever—male or female—to lace up sneakers. After she was the top high school player in her home state of New York, she was the national player of the year with the University of Connecticut in 2002. She joined the Seattle Storm and won the first of her four WNBA titles in 2004. That trophy came after she had led the United States to a gold medal in the 2004 Summer Olympics. She would repeat that feat four more times to become the only person ever with four pro league titles and five Olympic championships in hoops. The great Bird of the WNBA flew into retirement after the 2022 season, knowing someone will have to go a long way to top her marks.

SUPER STAT

13

THE NUMBER OF WNBA ALL-STAR GAMES THAT BIRD PLAYED IN DURING HER 19-YEAR CAREER, ALL WITH SEATTLE

Who won back-to-back NBA Finals MVPs in 2017 and 2018?

S ometimes it's just a matter of landing in the right place at the right time—and coming through in the clutch. That's what **KEVIN DURANT** did when he joined the Golden State Warriors before the 2016–17 season. KD was already an NBA superstar, a four-time league scoring champion while with the Oklahoma City Thunder. He had been the 2008 NBA Rookie of the Year with the Seattle SuperSonics, who moved to Oklahoma City the following season. In 2014, Durant was the NBA MVP as well. But he had never grabbed the big ring as an NBA champ. He proved to be the key piece missing from the Warriors, and he teamed with Stephen Curry and Klay Thompson to form an unbeatable scoring machine. In the 2017 NBA Finals, Durant was the top scorer, even as LeBron James tried to steer the Cleveland Cavaliers to another title. Durant won his own first championship and the NBA Finals MVP. The Warriors beat the Cavaliers again in 2018 and Durant was named NBA Finals MVP for the second time.

SUPER STAT

3

PLAYERS WITH TWO MVP TROPHIES
BEFORE AGE 26: ANTETOKOUNMPO,
MICHAEL JORDAN, AND
KAREEM ABDUL-JABBAR

Who was the NBA Finals MVP from Greece who led Milwaukee to the 2021 NBA title?

The championship story of **GIANNIS ANTETOKOUNMPO** reads almost like a fairy tale. The son of Nigerian immigrants to Greece, the future superstar grew up poor, often having to work as a youngster to help support his family. But as he grew (and grew!), he became a basketball star. He was good enough to be chosen by the Milwaukee Bucks in the 2013 NBA Draft, though he had never played with a school team, only clubs in Greece. Long, lean, and very hard-working, Antetokounmpo soon made an impact. In 2016–17, he finished in the NBA's top 20 in five different statistics: points, rebounds, assists, blocks, and steals. No other player had ever done that! By 2019, he won the first of his back-to-back NBA MVP awards, adding the Defensive Player of the Year trophy in 2020 as well. The 2020–21 season was his most successful to date, however. He set a career-high to that point by averaging 28.1 points per game. He led the Bucks to the team's first NBA Finals appearance since 1974 (they won their only other title in 1971). But Milwaukee lost the first two games to the Phoenix Suns and it looked like the dream season would end in disappointment. Antetokounmpo put his team on his shoulders and dominated. He led all players in points and rebounds, Milwaukee won the last four games in a row, and the kid from Greece was the NBA Finals MVP.

These players left their marks on and off the court

COOL CHA

ACTERS

FAST FACT: The third overall pick in 2009, Harden became the first player ever drafted by the Oklahoma City Thunder. The team had relocated from Seattle after the 2008 NBA Draft.

Who inspires "Fear the Beard" signs at games?

When he was a sophomore at Arizona State, **JAMES HARDEN** decided he wasn't going to shave anymore. Since then, opposing players have had plenty of reason to "fear the beard." Harden is one of basketball's most savvy scorers. He's a great ball-handler with an uncanny feel for getting defenders off-balance. And his lefthanded shooting stroke is one of the prettiest in the NBA.

Harden was an All-America player in 2008–09, and in '09 was drafted third overall by the Oklahoma City Thunder. He proved to be the missing piece for the Thunder, who had young stars in Kevin Durant and Russell Westbrook but had not made the playoffs since relocating to Oklahoma City from Seattle. In 2009–10, the Thunder made the playoffs, and Harden quickly developed into one of the game's best scorers. In 2011–12, he won NBA Sixth Man of the Year honors and helped the Thunder reach the NBA Finals. By 2017–18, he had won the first of three consecutive league scoring titles; he was also the NBA MVP that season. In 2018–19, he averaged a career-high 36.1 points per game. The Beard has been chosen for the NBA All-Star Game every season since 2012–13.

SUPER STAT

61

CAREER-HIGH SINGLE-GAME SCORING TOTAL BY HARDEN IN A JANUARY 2019 GAME AGAINST THE NEW YORK KNICKS

Who was known as the "Iceman"?

His calm, cool demeanor and his incredible skills on the court made the Iceman the perfect nickname for **GEORGE GERVIN**.

Gervin, a 6´7˝ swingman who often attacked from the perimeter, was a terrific scorer. His go-to shot was the finger roll. Gervin would glide toward the basket and sink finger rolls from as far out as the free-throw line. Gervin played most of his career with the San Antonio Spurs, winning four scoring titles and making 12 All-Star teams.

Early in the 1981–82 season, Gervin missed a week of games while nursing a thigh injury. His replacement, Ron Brewer, scored 39, 40, and 44 points in the three games Gervin missed. In his first game back, Gervin scored 47 points. Afterward, Gervin was asked if his play was motivated by possibly losing his starting job. His answer? "Ice be cool."

FAST FACT: The Gasol brothers were teammates on Spain's national team that won the 2006 FIBA World Championship.

Who are the only brothers to be traded for each other?

After winning three straight titles from 1999–2000 through 2001–02, the Los Angeles Lakers went into a championship drought. So midway through the '07–08 season, L.A. made a blockbuster trade for an All-Star big man: they acquired **PAU GASOL** from the Memphis Grizzlies. In return, the Grizzlies got two first-round picks, some young players, and a former Lakers second-round pick who had been playing in Europe. That player had a familiar name: **MARC GASOL**. Pau and Marc are the only brothers in the NBA ever to be traded for each other.

The trade ended up benefiting both teams. In Pau's first three seasons with the Lakers, they went to the NBA Finals three times, winning it twice. Meanwhile, Marc, at 6´11˝, developed into an All-Star for the Grizzlies and won NBA Defensive Player of the Year honors in '12–13.

Who is the shortest player in NBA history?

It's difficult for a small player to contribute in the NBA, which is why it was so amazing that **MUGGSY BOGUES** played for 14 seasons. At 5′ 3″, he is the shortest player to ever play in the league. Bogues starred in college at Wake Forest University, where his No. 14 jersey is retired. He won the Frances Pomeroy Naismith Award, given to the most outstanding senior who is 6′ 0″ or shorter, for the 1986–87 season.

Bogues went on to become an excellent playmaker at the NBA level. He played his rookie season with the Washington Bullets, who drafted him 12th overall in 1987. They did not protect his rights, however, so he ended up heading to the Charlotte Hornets in the 1988 expansion draft. Bogues went on to be a longtime starter for the Hornets. He had two seasons in which he averaged more than 10 assists per game and was a pest on defense with 1.5 steals per game over the course of his career.

SUPER STAT

39

CAREER BLOCKS MADE BY BOGUES, INCLUDING A REMARKABLE ONE ON A SHOT ATTEMPTED BY 7' 0" PATRICK EWING

FAST FACT: Muresan starred alongside actor Billy Crystal in the 1998 film *My Giant*.

Who was the tallest player in NBA history?

Born in Romania, **GHEORGHE MURESAN** was listed at 7′7″, making him the tallest player in the history of the NBA. Manute Bol was also listed at that height, but it is widely believed that Muresan had at least a half an inch over him. Muresan was drafted by the Washington Bullets in the second round of the 1993 NBA Draft. Muresan played only 310 games in the NBA, but he was an effective player when he stayed healthy. Over the course of his career, he blocked 1.5 shots per game. In 1995–96, he blocked 2.3 shots per game while averaging 14.5 points and 9.6 rebounds. He was named the NBA's Most Improved Player that season. Muresan continued to play professional basketball overseas after his NBA career came to an end.

Who was known as Dr. J?

When **JULIUS ERVING** was playing basketball at Roosevelt High School in New York, he and friend Leon Saunders had nicknames for each other. Erving called Saunders the Professor, and Saunders called Erving the Doctor. Soon, everyone started calling him Dr. Julius, which was shortened to Dr. J.

A 6´7″ forward, Erving would glide to the basket and, with his incredible vertical leap, hang in the air. Playing for the University of Massachusetts, he averaged an amazing 26.3 points and 20.2 rebounds in two seasons. He joined the ABA's New York Nets in 1973 and went on to win the league's MVP award three times while leading the Nets to two titles.

After the ABA merged with the NBA for the 1976–77 season, the Philadelphia 76ers traded for Erving's contract, and Dr. J became a star in Philly. He was the league's MVP in 1980–81 and led Philly to a title in '82–83.

SUPER STAT

657

CAREER STEALS MADE
BY SWOOPES, FIFTH-MOST
ON THE WNBA'S
ALL-TIME LIST

Who was the first female player to have a Nike shoe named after her?

Playing college basketball at Texas Tech, **SHERYL SWOOPES** burst onto the national scene with one of the greatest big-game performances ever. She led the Lady Raiders to the 1993 NCAA title by scoring 47 points in the final, the most ever in a men's or women's title game. A 6-foot forward, she was skilled, gritty, and aggressive on the court.

But there was no U.S. professional league for her to compete in after that season. It wasn't until 1997 when the WNBA was born that Swoopes joined the Houston Comets as the league's first player. She took the court midway through the season, six weeks after giving birth to her son.

Swoopes had another first in '95: She became the first female player to have a Nike signature shoe. Swoopes helped the Comets win the WNBA championship in each of the league's first four years. She played in the league into her 40s, making six All-Star game appearances and becoming the league's first three-time MVP.

FAST FACT: Playing for the Comets on July 27, 1999, Swoopes recorded the first triple-double in WNBA history: 14 points, 15 rebounds, and 10 assists against the Detroit Shock.

Who was known simply as "Magic"?

Since **EARVIN JOHNSON** first jumped onto the national stage at Michigan State, only his mother and a few friends and family called him Earvin. To the sports world, he was and is . . . Magic. He earned the nickname in high school, and made it famous when he led Michigan State to the 1979 NCAA title. As a rookie with the Lakers in 1980, he led them to the first of five NBA titles he would with the team. A dazzling passer, he remade the point guard position with his size and creativity, leading the NBA in assists per game five times. He won three NBA MVP awards and earned the NBA Finals award three times as well. In 1991, he announced that he has the HIV virus. Other than a brief 1996 comeback, he did not play again, but his legacy as one of the NBA's all-time greats is secure.

SUPER STAT

42

POINTS MAGIC SCORED IN GAME 6 OF THE 1980 FINALS, WHEN HE PLAYED CENTER AFTER KAREEM ABDUL-JABBAR WAS INJURED

Who won two WNBA Finals MVP awards with Minnesota?

One of the most decorated and successful WNBA players of all time, **SYLVIA FOWLES** has been setting a high standard since she joined the Chicago Sky in 2008. She was twice the Defensive Player of the Year with Chicago. She moved to the Minnesota Lynx in 2015 and helped them win WNBA championships in 2015 and 2017. Her great defensive play and outstanding rebounding ability helped her win the MVP for both of those WNBA Finals. She's not done year, having added two more DPOY trophies in 2016 and 2021.

What exciting star was the 2020 WNBA MVP?

Las Vegas Aces star **A'JA WILSON** was a hometown star made very, very good. A native of South Carolina, she stayed in-state to lead the University of South Carolina to the 2017 national championship. She was the school's first four-time All-America as well. Wilson continued her success after joining the Aces as the first overall draft pick in 2018. A 20.7 points-per-game average helped her win the Rookie of the Year award, and she earned her first WNBA MVP award in 2020. The only tough part of her great 2020 season was a 3–0 series loss to the Seattle Storm in the WNBA Finals. Wilson remains one of the WNBA's best overall players, combining shooting skills, leadership, and speed. The 2020 trophy probably won't be her last!

SUPER STAT

2

NUMBER OF PLAYERS TO LEAD THE
NBA IN TOTAL POINTS AND ASSISTS.
YOUNG JOINS NATE ARCHIBALD
ON THIS SHORT LIST

Who was the first player ever with 45 points and 10 assists in a conference finals game?

The Dallas Mavericks chose **TRAE YOUNG** in the first round of the 2018 NBA Draft after his dominant single season at Oklahoma. Then they traded Young to Atlanta for Luca Doncic. So far, that's looking like a trade working well for both teams. Young was one of the NBA's top rookies before averaging a career-high 29.6 points per game in 2019–20. He had dazzling moves, an ability to be daring in drives to the hoop, and creativity in passing that made his teammates b etter. In 2021, he led the Hawks to the playoffs, where his skills got an even bigger audience. In the first two rounds, he averaged better than 29 points per game, but that was just a signal of bigger things to come. In Game 1 of the Eastern Conference Finals against Giannis Antetokounmpo and the Milwaukee Bucks, Young poured in 48 points and dished out 11 assists. No one had ever done that in an NBA conference final game. Add in division finals, and Young was the youngest ever to reach 40 points and 10 assists in a conference finals game, nipping LeBron James by a few months. It was also the most points scored by a player in his first conference finals game as well. Unfortunately, the Hawks lost the series in six games. But the standout performance—along with his many highlight-reel plays—signaled that the NBA has a new star on the rise.

FAST FACT: Including high school, college, and his first four NBA seasons, Young has averaged less than 20 points per game only once—his 2018–19 rookie season, when he was still pretty close at 19.1.

41

Who was the tallest player to play in an NBA All-Star game?

The NBA had seen giants like the 7′ 6″ **YAO MING** before: Gheorghe Muresan (7′ 7″), Manute Bol (7′ 7″), and Shawn Bradley (7′ 6″). All of them were role players in the NBA—but Yao was different. The top pick of the 2002 NBA NBA Draft out of China, Yao had the kind of athleticism, strength, and coordination rarely seen in 7-footers.

Yao didn't score a single point in his NBA debut. But a few weeks later he started piling up points, 20 against the Los Angeles Lakers and 30 against the Dallas Mavericks. By midseason he was a double-double machine and was elected to start the All-Star Game as a rookie, the tallest player ever to play in the game. Yao made the All-Star team in each of his eight NBA seasons.

But with the Chinese national team running him through a grueling schedule every offseason, he missed the entire 2009–10 NBA season with a foot injury. He tried to come back a year later, but was forced to retire after just five games. His NBA career wasn't long, but it was great.

2016

YEAR THAT YAO MING WAS ELECTED TO THE BASKETBALL HALL OF FAME FOR HIS NBA AND INTERNATIONAL CAREERS

Who was called "Air Canada" for his dunking skills?

The Toronto Raptors joined the NBA in 1995, but they really soared into league when **VINCE CARTER** joined the team for the 1998–99 season. He played with the Raptors for most of seven seasons, averaging 20 or more points five times and earning five All-Star Game selections. But it was one evening in February 2000 that turned Carter into a legend. His display in the NBA Slam Dunk Contest is still talked about as one of the greatest ever—more than 20 years later. Carter opened with a reverse windmill 360 that brought the crowd in Oakland to its feet. His fellow players' jaws dropped in amazement. He followed that with a windmill from behind the backboard. His next dunk came after he caught a bounce pass and then went through his legs before slamming the ball home. In the final round, he hung on the rim with his elbow after a slam. His last dunk was with two hands from near the free-throw line! "Air Canada" was the high-flying contest winner!

SUPER STAT

8

NUMBER OF NBA TEAMS VINCE CARTER PLAYED FOR IN HIS 22-YEAR NBA CAREER, WHICH ENDED IN 2020

Who was the only player with more blocked shots than points in an NBA career?

In the 1983 NBA Draft, the San Diego Clippers picked **MANUTE BOL** despite the fact that they had never seen him play. Why? Because the center from Sudan was 7′7″ tall! Bol never played for San Diego—he was declared ineligible for the draft—but two years later, the Washington Bullets selected him in the second round. Bol went on to play 10 seasons in the NBA, mostly as a back up. Despite being very thin, his height made him a defensive force. He blocked 15 shots in a game twice, and blocked eight shots in a quarter twice, tying an NBA record. Bol finished his career with 2,086 blocks, far more than the number of points he scored (1,599).

Who was the first woman to be head coach in an NBA game?

On December 30, 2020, San Antonio Spurs head coach Gregg Popovich was ejected from the game. That was not a big deal; "Pop" has been kicked out nearly 20 times. What was a big deal was the assistant coach he turned to lead the team for the rest of the game. Taking over as interim head coach, and making NBA history, was **BECKY HAMMON**, the first woman to hold that job . . . if only for a short time. Hammon was used to firsts. In 2013, a knee injury ended Hammon's successful 16-season WNBA career. In 2014 she was the first woman to be named a full-time assistant coach. Hammon went on to coach the Spurs summer-league teams, too. After eight seasons with San Antonio, she returned to the WNBA to be head coach of the Las Vegas Aces for the 2022 season.

FAST FACT: Wade was at his best in the big games. In the 2006 NBA Finals, he started Miami's great comeback from being down 0–2 by scoring 42 points, including 15 in the fourth quarter, to win Game 3 over Dallas.

What three-time NBA champion was known as "Flash"?

When three-time NBA champ Shaquille O'Neal arrived in Miami in 2004, he saw the potential in second-year guard **DWYANE WADE**, who had been the Heat's No. 1 pick in the 2003 NBA Draft. To encourage the younger player, O'Neal nicknamed Wade "Flash." "At first," Wade said later, "I didn't like it!" But the speed-inspired name was just right for the multitalented Wade, whose court movement for a player of his size left defenses gasping. Teaming with O'Neal's inside skills, Wade led the Miami Heat to the team's first NBA title in 2006. The Heat lost the first two games of that finals series to Dallas, but Wade was then the top scorer in four straight wins, earning the NBA Finals MVP award. In 2009, Wade led the NBA in scoring. History repeated itself in 2010–11. Another superstar, former Cleveland Cavalier LeBron James, joined Miami along with talented forward Chris Bosh. Teamed with Wade, the trio dominated the East and led the Heat to a pair of NBA titles in 2012 and 2013. After brief stints with Chicago and Cleveland, Wade returned to Miami to close out his 16-year career where it all started on South Beach. His next stop will surely be Springfield, Massachusetts, home of the Naismith Memorial Basketball Hall of Fame.

SUPER STAT

1

DWYANE WADE'S RANK ON THE MIAMI HEAT ALL-TIME CAREER LISTS FOR GAMES, POINTS, ASSISTS, AND STEALS

Who was often referred to as the Human Highlight Film?

During the 1980s, the high-flying Michael Jordan took the NBA by storm. There was only one player who could stand toe-to-toe with Jordan when it came to throwing down dunks: Atlanta Hawks star **DOMINIQUE WILKINS**.

Wilkins was all about power. He would leap off of two feet, coming to a stop before unloading ferocious dunks, often his signature windmill. Those eye-popping slams earned him a fitting nickname: Human Highlight Film.

Wilkins was more than just a dunker, though. A nine-time All-Star, he was a skilled scorer who led the league in points per game (30.3) in 1985–86. In 2006, he was inducted into the Basketball Hall of Fame.

FAST FACT: Nneka (2012) and Chiney ('14) each won the WNBA's Rookie of the Year award.

Who were the only siblings to be drafted first overall?

Sisters **NNEKA** and **CHINEY OGWUMIKE** aren't twins, though their accomplishments on the basketball court have been nearly identical. They both played at Cypress-Fairbanks High School in Texas, where they each were named the Gatorade girls' basketball national player of the year (Nneka in 2008, Chiney in 2010). They both played for Stanford, where they were named Pac-12 Player of the Year twice (Nneka in 2010 and '12, Chiney in 2013 and '14).

They both were selected first overall in the WNBA Draft—Nneka by the Los Angeles Sparks in 2012; Chiney by the Connecticut Sun in 2014. They're the only pair of siblings to each be drafted first overall in the NBA or WNBA drafts. On July 13, 2014, the siblings faced each other as opponents for the first time. Nneka led the Sparks to the win. They've been Sparks teammates since 2019.

What defensive star is known as the "Stifle Tower"?

To understand this interesting NBA nickname, you have to know a little bit about French history. The Eiffel Tower stands 984 feet tall in Paris, France, where it has been the centerpiece of the city since it was built in 1889. In 2013, 124 years later, another towering French landmark made a big impact on the NBA, and writers quickly dubbed **RUDY GOBERT** the "Stifle Tower." Stifle means to stop, prevent, or delay, and the 7'1" Gobert quickly showed that he was one of the top shot-blockers in the game. Gobert first played for a pro team in France before he joined the Jazz in 2013. He led the NBA in total blocks in 2017 and 2021, and in rebounds in 2020 and 2021. He has earned three Defensive Player of the Year awards (2018, 2019, 2021), tied for second most all-time. He's no slouch on offense, leading the NBA three times in field-goal percentage. The highlight of Gobert's long international career with France was a silver medal at the 2020 Summer Olympics, the best finish ever by that nation.

SUPER STAT

3

NUMBER OF TIMES THAT RUDY GOBERT LED THE NBA IN FIELD-GOAL PERCENTAGE

What all-around star won his first NBA title with the Lakers in 2020?

Heading into the 2019–20 season, there was very little that **ANTHONY DAVIS** had not accomplished in his NBA career. He was a three-time NBA blocked-shot champ, a seven-time NBA All-Star, and had six seasons averaging more than 24 points per game, while earning spots on several NBA All-Defensive teams. What was missing? A ring. Davis had been a breakout, one-season star at Kentucky in 2011–12, where he won a stack of national player of the year honors while leading the Wildcats to the national title (plus picking a memorable nickname, Unibrow, after his distinctive eyebrows). He began his pro career as the No. 1 overall pick by the New Orleans Hornets in 2012 (they became the Pelicans a season later). He quickly showed he was among the league's elite, not only leading in blocks, but also in two-point baskets three times. His 6'10" size and great inside moves made him a dominant player in the paint. Though he helped the U.S. win the 2012 Olympic gold medal, Davis and New Orleans only made the postseason twice during his seven seasons there. In search of that elusive ring, Davis moved to the Lakers to join LeBron James. He led Los Angeles with a 26.1 points per game and 9.3 rebounds per game. The talented Lakers swarmed over their opponents in the playoffs, losing only three games on their way to the NBA Finals against **JIMMY BUTLER** and the Miami Heat. There, the duo of A.D. and The King proved to be too much. The Lakers won in six games and Davis had his long-looked-for championship ring. Davis scored more points in that postseason than any other player, including James. He also became the first player to win championships in college, the NBA, the Olympics, and the FIBA World Cup (2014).

SUPER STAT

26.89

CAREER PLAYER EFFICIENCY RATING FOR ANTHONY DAVIS, FOURTH ALL-TIME IN NBA HISTORY THROUGH THE 2022 SEASON

Who was the first Australian-born player to win Rookie of the Year?

red Irving was a star at Boston University in the 1980s, finishing his career as the school's all-time leading scorer. He went on to play professionally with the Bulleen Boomers in Australia. While he was playing there in 1992, his wife gave birth to a son, **KYRIE IRVING**.

The Irvings moved back to the U.S. when Kyrie was 2 years old. He was a top recruit for Duke University, and despite an injury-filled freshman year, he declared for the 2011 NBA Draft. The Cleveland Cavaliers took him with the top pick. Irving shined for the Cavs in his first season. He led all rookies in scoring (18.5 points per game) and averaged a team-high 5.4 assists per game. He was named the NBA Rookie of the Year. He has since earned seven NBA All-Star Game selections. (Note: In 2018, **BEN SIMMONS** joined Irving as an Australian-born NBA Rookie of the Year.)

Who was the shortest player to lead the NBA in rebounding?

Typically, the best rebounders are also the tallest players. But that was never the case with NBA legend **CHARLES BARKLEY**. He was known as the Round Mound of Rebound because of his unusual build: Depending on whom you believe, Barkley was somewhere between 6′4″ and 6′6″, meaning he was sometimes half a foot shorter than the players he was battling on the boards. He also had the kind of thick build you'd expect to see on a football field, not a basketball court.

So how is it that Barkley, in his third NBA season, became the shortest player to lead the NBA in rebounding when he grabbed 14.6 boards per game for the Philadelphia 76ers in 1986–87? For one, he was really strong. He easily cleared out space around the basket. He was also deceivingly athletic, with a feel for where missed shots would bounce. But most of all, he was tenacious. A young Barkley was a ball of energy, outworking taller players for all those boards. That season was anything but a fluke. During his 16-season Hall of Fame career, Barkley averaged double-digit rebounds 15 times.

RECORD B

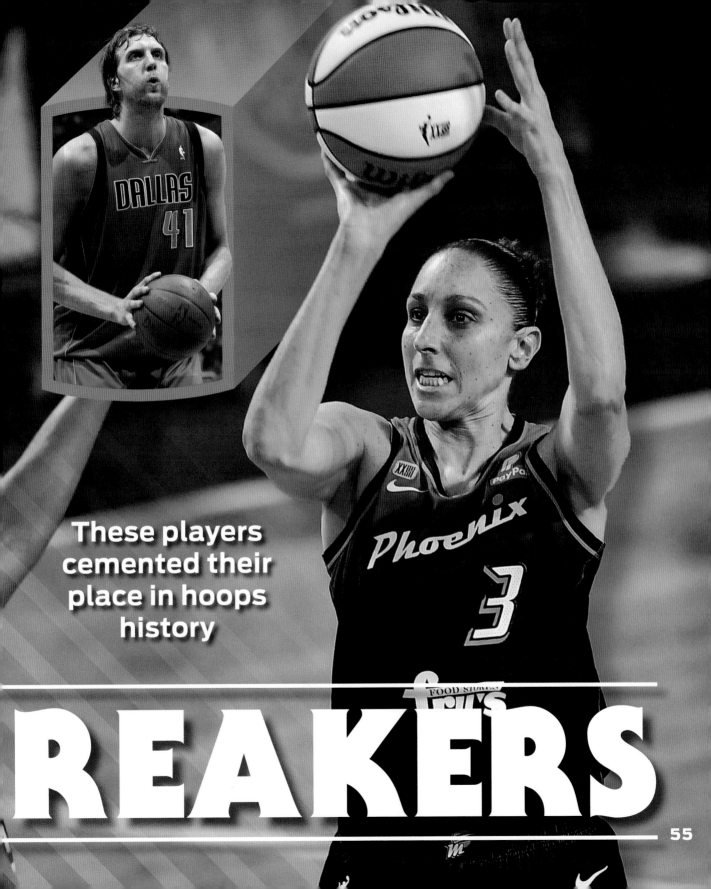

These players cemented their place in hoops history

REAKERS

10:49
17

TISSOT

88:88

PROTECT

162

NCAA-RECORD THREE-POINTERS
MADE BY CURRY DURING
2007–08 SEASON AT DAVIDSON

In 2021, who broke the NBA career record for three-pointers?

The answer to this question will come as no surprise to anyone who has watched basketball in the past decade-plus. On December 14, 2021, **STEPHEN CURRY** drained his 2,794th three-pointer, breaking the previous all-time mark set by **RAY ALLEN**. By the end of the 2021–22 season, Curry had extended his own record to 3,117. The career mark joins a host of shooting and scoring marks the superstar guard has set. His 402 treys in 2015–16 are the single-season record (breaking his own previous record of 286 a year earlier). His shooting skills have helped him lead the NBA in three-pointers seven times, win two NBA scoring titles, and earn the 2015 and 2016 NBA MVP awards. Perhaps more importantly to Curry, however, are the four NBA championships he has helped the Golden State Warriors win. Needless to say, he is the NBA Finals all-time leader with 152 three-pointers. In 2022, Curry added yet another page to his incredible record book by earning his first NBA Finals MVP trophy.

Who played in the most career NBA games?

When it comes to having a long and memorable NBA career, no one can top big man **ROBERT PARISH**. Parish played in a record 1,611 games in a career that spanned 21 seasons and four championships. The 7′1″, 250-pound center was known for his defense and high-arcing jumper. He averaged double-digits in points for 17 straight seasons from 1977–78 through '93–94 and was a nine-time All-Star.

Parish is most remembered for his 14 seasons with the Boston Celtics. Parish and teammates Larry Bird and **KEVIN McHALE** were nicknamed the Big Three for their dominance, as they led the Celtics to titles in 1980–81, '83–84, and '85–86. (Parish's fourth championship came with the Chicago Bulls in the final season of his career.)

SUPER STAT

10

NUMBER OF NBA SEASONS IN WHICH ROBERT PARISH AVERAGED AT LEAST 10 REBOUNDS PER GAME

Who set the WNBA record for points in a game?

On July 17, 2018, **LIZ CAMBAGE** of the Dallas Wings started scoring against the New York Liberty ... and didn't stop! The star center from Australia poured in bucket after bucket, posting up for layups, draining threes, and burying free throws. When the final buzzer sounded, Cambage had 53 points, breaking the WNBA record by two points. She made 4 out of 5 three-point attempts, and was 15 of 16 from the line. From the field, including threes, she shot an incredible 77 percent! She also had 10 rebounds so it was a double-double as well. Cambage had played two WNBA seasons in 2011 and 2013, before returning to play pro in China and Australia. She joined the Wings in 2018. After two seasons with Las Vegas, she played part of the 2022 season with the Los Angeles Sparks.

Who broke the NBA mark for most points in one quarter?

On January 23, 2015, Golden State Warriors shooting guard **KLAY THOMPSON** was unstoppable, scoring 52 points, with 11 three-pointers, to beat the Sacramento Kings 126–101. What he did in the third quarter was truly brilliant: He went 13 for 13 from the field, including nine three-pointers (the most ever in a quarter), and totaled a record-shattering 37 points in the period. A sharpshooter with a picture-perfect release, the 6′ 6″ Thompson was the 11th overall pick in the 2011 NBA Draft and named to the NBA All-Rookie First Team in 2012. He played in his first All-Star Game in 2015. Thompson and guard Stephen Curry formed the Warriors backcourt nicknamed the "Splash Brothers" for their dazzling playmaking and amazing shooting abilities.

FAST FACT: Another trophy fact for Sue Bird's household: Her fiancée, Megan Rapinoe, won two Women's World Cup titles in 2015 and 2019.

Who won WNBA titles in three different decades?

After she retired following the 2022 WNBA season, **SUE BIRD** had plenty of time to build a trophy case. And she's going to need a BIG one! Few players in any sport have earned as many championships as this multitalented guard. After winning a pair of NCAA titles with Connecticut, she joined the Seattle Storm in 2002. With the only WNBA team she would ever play for, Bird won WNBA championships in 2004 (2000s), 2010 and 2018 (2010s), and 2020 (2020s), the only player to win titles in three different decades. Achieving that meant not only excelling on the court, but also understanding the need for fitness and focus to return year after year. Even with all that WNBA work, Bird had time to put together an amazing international record. She was part of a record-tying five Olympic gold-medal-winning teams for the United States (2004, '08, '12, '16, and '20). Bird also led the U.S. team to victory at four FIBA World Cup tournaments.

Who had the most assists in an NBA game?

O n December 30, 1990, Orlando Magic point guard **SCOTT SKILES** made history against the Denver Nuggets when he dished out a jaw-dropping 30 assists, the highest single-game total in NBA history. The 6′1″ point guard had more than twice as many assists as the Nuggets' team total (14). He also scored 22 points to lead the Magic to a 155–116 win.

Although Skiles was an NBA journeyman who never played in an All-Star Game, he left his mark. While at Michigan State, Skiles was the Big Ten Player of the Year in 1986. He was also the NBA's Most Improved Player in 1991 with the Magic. His basketball savvy allowed him to become a head coach after his playing days, leading the Phoenix Suns, Chicago Bulls, Orlando Magic, and Milwaukee Bucks.

Who played in the most NBA All-Star Games?

You could make the argument that **KAREEM ABDUL-JABBAR** is the greatest to ever play the game. He is certainly the most decorated. No player in NBA history has ever scored more points (38,387), won more MVP awards (six), or made more All-Star appearances (19). Abdul-Jabbar also played the game with unmatched grace at the big man's position.

Born Lew Alcindor (Abdul-Jabbar changed his name before the 1971–72 season), he led the UCLA Bruins to three national titles and was a two-time National Player of the Year. The Milwaukee Bucks selected him with the first pick in the 1969 NBA Draft, and he was immediately the most imposing center in the league, winning Rookie of the Year honors his first season. After one NBA title and three MVP awards with the Bucks, Abdul-Jabbar was traded to the Los Angeles Lakers in 1975. He helped lead the Lakers to five championships. With his signature skyhook, Abdul-Jabbar changed the game and sealed his legacy as one of the NBA's all-time greats.

FAST FACT: Rodman earned the nickname the Worm as a kid because of the way he wriggled while playing pinball.

Who led the league in rebounding the most consecutive seasons?

With his colorful hairstyles and fierce playing style, the 6′7″, 220-pound forward **DENNIS RODMAN** was always easy to spot on the court. But it would often seem like he was coming out of nowhere to crash the boards to grab rebound after rebound. Rodman had a knack for locating the ball once it was shot and outworked opponents, making him a seven-time NBA rebounding champion. He led the league in boards per game for seven consecutive seasons (1991–92 through 1997–98). His elite rebounding ability made Rodman a key part of five championship teams (the Detroit Pistons in 1989 and '90 and the Chicago Bulls in '96, '97, and '98). Legendary players Isiah Thomas and Michael Jordan stole the spotlight during those championship runs, but it was Rodman's hustle on both ends of the floor that helped those squads win titles. A two-time All-Star and seven-time member of the All-Defensive First Team, Rodman was also named the NBA Defensive Player of the Year twice (1989–90 and '90–91).

Who was the first NBA player to average a triple-double for a season?

Talk about a good start to your NBA career. **OSCAR ROBERTSON** debuted in 1960 with the Cincinnati Royals. In his second season, he averaged 30.8 points, 12.5 rebounds, and 11.4 assists per game, a triple-double that was not duplicated by anyone until 2017 by Russell Westbrook. "The Big O" had a great start and his career ended well—in the Hall of Fame.

FAST FACT: Eaton blocked 3,064 shots as a member of the Utah Jazz, a franchise record.

Who blocked the most shots in an NBA season?

Center **MARK EATON** never averaged double-digit points per game during his 11-year career. But his focus was on the defensive end, where he will forever be remembered as one of the best rim protectors the NBA has ever seen. During the 1984–85 NBA season, he blocked 456 shots, an NBA record for most blocks in a season. Eaton blocked an amazing 5.6 shots per game that year. The 7′ 4″, 290-pound center spent his entire career as a member of the Utah Jazz. He was a two-time NBA Defensive Player of the Year (1984–85 and '88–89) and made the All-Defensive First Team three times. Eaton led the league in blocks four times in his career. He also was tops in the league in defensive rebounds in 1984–85 with 720.

1

Who was the first WNBA player in the 50-40-90 club?

When **ELENA DELLE DONNE** was named the 2013 WNBA Rookie of the Year, she joined a long list of star players. When she won the scoring title in 2015, she was again on a strong list. When she earned her second WNBA MVP in 2019, she was on a shorter list, but she was still not alone. When she led the Washington Mystics to the 2019 WNBA championship, she finally got her ring, joining the league's long history of superstar champions. But that same season, she put her name on a list of one. Her performance that season made Delle Donne the only WNBA player to average better than 50 percent (51.5) from the field, and above 40 percent (43.0) from three-point land, AND 90-plus form the line (97.4). She joins eight NBA players in the 50-40-90 club, but no other WNBA player is on there with her. The former Delaware All-American played four seasons with the Chicago Sky before moving to the Mystics in 2017.

Who is the NBA's career leader in field-goal percentage?

What goes up, must go in. That's how veteran center **DeANDRE JORDAN** plays the game. The big man plays close to the basket, which helps increase his success, but no matter how close he gets, he still has to put the ball in the hoop. Jordan has done that better than any player in NBA history.

His 67.3 field-goal percentage sits atop the NBA career list. He led the league in five consecutive seasons—2013 to 2017. He also led in rebounds twice. That ability to get after the ball in the paint is what has made him so valuable to so many teams. Jordan joined the Los Angeles Clippers in 2008 as a second-round draft pick. He was a key part of the Clippers' rise in the early 2010s, which saw them make the playoffs six times in a row after missing them for five seasons. Jordan has never averaged as much as 13 points per game, but all of the points he does score come amid tall bodies, long-reaching arms, and fierce defense. He showed he had the ability to fight all of that off and score. After 10 seasons with the Clippers, he has spent short stints with five other teams, always bringing his strong inside game and a growing level of leadership later in his career.

FAST FACT: Jordan does more than shoot accurately. He led the NBA in rebounds-per-game average twice, and has averaged 13 or more rebounds per game in seven seasons.

Who first went 24-for-24 in free throws in one game?

During the Dallas Mavericks' 2010–11 championship run, star big man **DIRK NOWITZKI** was overpowering, with two 40-point performances and a 27.7 point-per-game average during the playoffs. Perhaps his most impressive feat came in Game 1 of the Western Conference finals against the Oklahoma City Thunder. Nowitzki went to the free-throw line 24 times—and made every shot, giving him the record for most free throws in a game without a miss. (James Harden later matched that feat in a 2019 game while with the Houston Rockets.) Nowitzki's cool at the line helped the Mavericks win and later and earn a spot in the NBA Finals. Led by Nowitzki, Dallas went on to upset the Miami Heat in six games, and Nowitzki took home the NBA Finals MVP award.

907

NBA

IRONMAN

NOV. 20, 1997

Who played in the most consecutive NBA games?

The grind of playing basketball at such a high level takes a toll on a player, so missing games due to injury happens often. That is why **A.C. GREEN**'s feat of 1,192 consecutive games played is so impressive.

Green was a 6′9″ forward who averaged 9.6 points and 7.4 rebounds per game in his career. He was a three-time NBA champion as a member of the Los Angeles Lakers (1986–87, '87–88, '99–2000) and an All-Star in 1990. Green was a gritty player and tough defender. On November 20, 1997, Green played in his 907th consecutive game. It was the most ever at the time and he went on to play 285 more through the end of the 2000–01 season. Green missed only three games his entire career, appearing in 1,278 of 1,280 games.

FAST FACT: Green starred at Oregon State University, where he was a three-time member of the All-Pac-10 First Team.

Who is the NBA's career leader in assists?

A point guard's job is to run the team's offense and make the players around him better. Few players in NBA history did that as well as **JOHN STOCKTON**, the league's all-time assist leader. The Utah Jazz selected Stockton with the 16th overall selection in the 1984 NBA Draft after being named the West Coast Conference Player of the Year as a senior at Gonzaga, averaging 20.9 points and 7.2 assists per game that season. When Stockton jumped to the NBA, his ability to see the floor was always on display. Stockton spent his entire career with the Jazz, and over the course of his 19 seasons in the NBA, he averaged 10.5 assists per game. In 1989–90, he had a career-high of 14.5 per game.

Stockton, a member of the original U.S. Dream Team that won gold at the 1992 Olympics, did most of his damage playing alongside one of the greatest forwards of all time, Karl Malone. On February 1, 1995, Malone received a bounce pass from Stockton and knocked down a baseline jumper. That assist helped Stockton surpass Magic Johnson as the NBA's all-time leader. Stockton didn't stop there. He finished his career with an astounding 15,806 assists before retiring after the 2002–03 season.

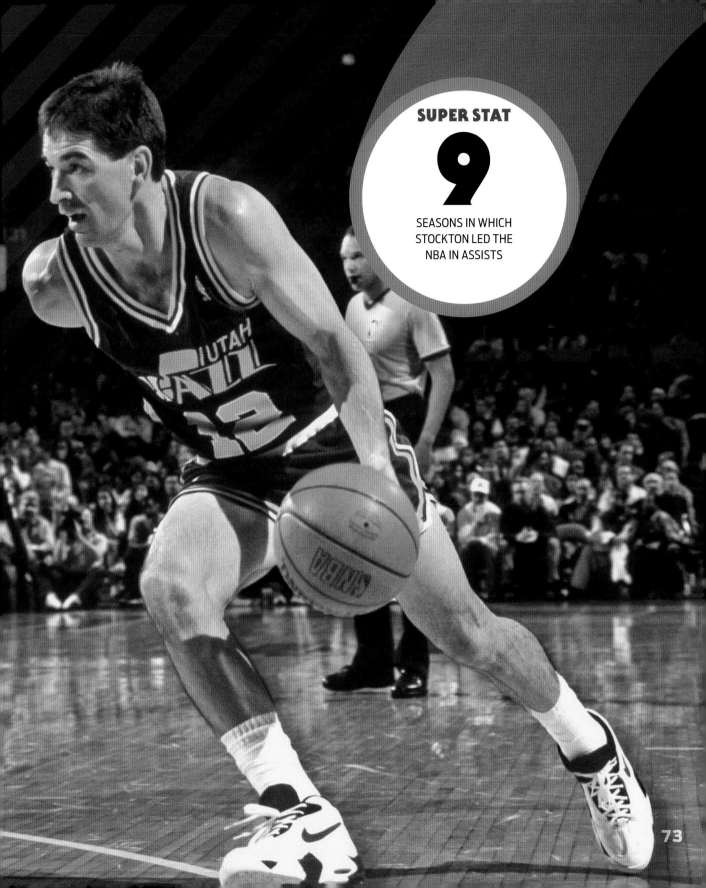

SUPER STAT

19.0

THE PER-GAME SCORING AVERAGE PIPPEN POSTED IN 35 NBA FINALS GAMES, HIS HIGHEST FOR ANY POSTSEASON ROUND

Who was the first player with two same-year NBA and Olympic titles?

The Chicago Bulls and Michael Jordan leaned heavily on the high-scoring forward **SCOTTIE PIPPEN** during the team's run of six championships in eight seasons. Pippen was a seven-time All-Star who paired with Jordan for highlight plays again and again. He was also one of the league's most ferocious defenders. He was on the NBA All-Defensive First Team eight times! Even as he was gathering rings with Chicago, Pippen was collecting gold with Team USA. He helped win the Olympic title in 1992 and 1996, two of the same seasons he won with the Bulls!

Who was the first teenager to score 150 points in a five-game stretch?

In the 2020 NBA Draft, the Minnesota Timberwolves chose wisely. The team made guard **ANTHONY EDWARDS** the top overall pick. Edwards, a star at Georgia, had a solid rookie season, third on the team with a 19.3 points-per-game average. Only 19, he became the fifth-youngest player to reach 1,000 career points; all the players ahead of him went on to multiple All-Star appearances. But his signature achievement came in a stunning five-game run in mid-March, 2021. In a game against the Pelicans, he poured in 27 points. In his next four games, he added 21, 34, 29, and 42 points. That last game against the Lakers made Edwards the youngest player in NBA history to score more than 150 points over a five-game stretch. He wound up leading his team in points as a rookie, too.

Who holds the NBA rookie three-point record?

Wait! Before you answer "Stephen Curry," read on! Curry had a NBA rookie record 166 threes in his rookie season in 2009–10. But **DAMIAN LILLARD** re-set the mark in 2013. Along came **DONOVAN MITCHELL** of the Utah Jazz. In the second-to-last game of the 2018 season, Mitchell hit four three-pointers. That gave him 186 for the season, topping Lillard's mark by one. The future All-Star then added another to make his final rookie-record total 187. Mitchell has been a huge part of Utah's six-season playoff streak, which began the year before Mitchell arrived in Salt Lake City. He led his team in scoring in each of his first five seasons.

Who is the WNBA's all-time leader in three-point shots?

Who is the WNBA's all-time scoring leader?
Who is the WNBA's all-time leader in made free throws?
Who is the WNBA's all-time leader in field goals of any kind?

The answer to all of these questions is the player already known around basketball as the GOAT: **DIANA TAURASI** . Since joining the WNBA's Phoenix Mercury in 2004 after a stellar career at Connecticut (three national titles, two seasons earning various player of the year awards), Taurasi has not stopped scoring. She was the 2004 WNBA Rookie of the Year and the 2009 WNBA MVP; she also won two WNBA Finals MVP awards (2009 and 2014) while helping the Mercury to three league titles. In 2017, she needed one three-point basket to become the league's all-time leader. Instead, she set a single-game record with eight, leaping past previous record-holder **KATIE SMITH** .

A few weeks later, she became the league's top scorer of all time. How good is she? In 2021, fans voted her the GOAT: Greatest of All Time . . . and she's still playing at the age of 40!

SUPER STAT

16

NUMBER OF SEASONS IN TAURASI'S
18-YEAR CAREER IN WHICH SHE HAS
AVERAGED AT LEAST
15.0 POINTS PER GAME

SUPER STAT

5

NBA-RECORD CONSECUTIVE SEASONS
IN WHICH HOWARD LED THE NBA IN
TOTAL REBOUNDS
(2005–06 TO '09–10)

Who was the tallest player to win a Slam Dunk Contest?

They say big guys never get respect in the NBA Slam Dunk contest because it's more exciting to see smaller players elevate and perform mid-air tricks. But with a 40-inch vertical leap, 6´11″ **DWIGHT HOWARD** could do all the things the little guys could, and then some. Before the 2008 contest, he came up with some of the most creative dunks the competition had ever seen. On one, Howard threw a toss from the left wing, leaped, tipped it off the backboard with his left hand, and then dunked it on the other side of the rim with his right.

But his signature dunk involved a costume. Howard took off his Orlando Magic jersey to reveal a Superman shirt, and he put on a red cape. He took off from just inside the free-throw line and soared so high up in the air that he threw the ball down through the hoop without touching the rim. He won the slam dunk title in a landslide, the tallest player ever to win it.

Howard's size, strength, and leaping ability make him the closest thing to a real-life Superman in the NBA. Those skills helped him become the first player to win the Defensive Player of the Year award three years in a row.

FAST FACT: In 2004–05, Howard became the first player to jump from high school to the NBA and play in all 82 games.

These players were
dangerous with the
ball in their hands

SUPER S

CORERS

FAST FACT: Kobe is a city in Japan that lends its name to a kind of beef. Bryant's parents were inspired to choose the name Kobe after seeing it on a restaurant menu.

HOWARD
12

Who scored the most points in a game since 1962?

On January 22, 2006, the Los Angeles Lakers were trailing the Toronto Raptors by 17 points in the third quarter. Annoyed at his team's performance, **KOBE BRYANT** took matters into his own hands. He scored 55 more points, adding to the 26 he already had, leading the Lakers to a 122–104 comeback win. Bryant's 81 points were the most since March 2, 1962, when Philadelphia Warriors center Wilt Chamberlain scored 100 points against the New York Knicks. Bryant finished the game with 28 made field goals, going 7-for-13 on three-pointers and 18-for-20 on free throws.

Bryant was drafted by the Charlotte Hornets 13th overall in 1996, but a deal had already been reached to send him to the Lakers. Since Bryant was only 17 at the time, his parents had to sign his contract. In the years that followed, Bryant developed into one of the game's all-time greats, setting a record with 18 straight All-Star selections. He won five championships with the Lakers, earned Finals MVP honors in 2009 and '10, led the NBA in scoring twice, and was named to the All-Defensive First Team nine times. In 2020, he was elected to the Basketball Hall of Fame, but it ended up being a sad ceremony; Bryant had been killed in a helicopter accident along with eight other people, including his daughter Gianna. Shortly after the superstar's death at age 41, the NBA All-Star Game MVP award was renamed in his honor.

SUPER STAT

50.4

CHAMBERLAIN'S ALL-TIME NBA-RECORD SCORING AVERAGE FOR THE 1961–62 SEASON

Who had the most 50-point games in NBA history?

The great **WILT CHAMBERLAIN** scored 50 or more points in a game a whopping 118 times. Nobody else in NBA history has reached that mark even 40 times. Chamberlain famously had 100 points on March 2, 1962, breaking his own single-game record of 78. He finished that season with 45 games in which he scored 50 or more points.

Chamberlain's dominant scoring ability led to rule changes. When Chamberlain was a college player at Kansas, his scoring ability was already legendary. Chamberlain had a reputation for taking a running start and dunking his foul shots, an idea so terrifying to the rest of the college basketball world that it was outlawed before he even appeared in a game.

Charles helped Connecticut win two NCAA titles, and Team USA win three Olympic gold medals.

Who won her second WNBA scoring title in 2021?

Who says 32 is too old in the WNBA? Younger players continue to arrive, but veteran **TINA CHARLES** continues to dominate. With the Washington Mystics in 2021, Charles averaged a league-best 23.4 points per game. She had won her first scoring title back in 2016 while with the New York Liberty. Since joining the WNBA in 2010 as the first overall pick by the Connecticut Sun, Charles has taken her talents to four other teams, consistently putting up points and minutes, while rarely missing games. Charles has made eight WNBA All-Star Games as well as earning the 2010 Rookie of the Year and 2012 MVP trophies. Her success at reaching the basket has made her fourth all-time in the WNBA in total points.

Who is the NBA's career leader in three-point percentage?

Guard **STEVE KERR** was a prolific long-range shooter for 15 NBA seasons, retiring in 2003 having made 45.4 percent of his three-pointers. Kerr earned a reputation as an elite shooter in college at Arizona, where as a senior he shot 57.3 percent from deep.

In the NBA, Kerr was a valuable role player, winning five championships. He played for the Chicago Bulls during their title runs from 1996 to '98. In Game 6 of the 1997 Finals against the Utah Jazz, Kerr hit the title-winning shot with five seconds left. After being traded in 1999 to the San Antonio Spurs, Kerr helped his new team to the 1999 title. He's not a bad coach, either, leading. the Golden State Warriors to four NBA titles.

Who averaged a triple-double four times?

All-time superstar Oscar "The Big O" Robertson did it first, but only **RUSSELL WESTBROOK** has put in four full seasons in which he averaged double figures in points, rebounds, and assists. In fact, in his 14-year career through 2022, Westbrook has redefined the stat and made it his own. In 2016–17, with the Houston Rockets, Westbrook matched the Big O's 1961–62 season. The following year, Westbrook did it again—and then again in 2018–19 for an incredible three consecutive seasons with double digits thrice! To prove it was not just the team he was on, Westbrook made it triple-double season No. 4 with the Washington Wizards in 2020–21, while also again leading the NBA in assists per game for the third time. In 2019, he had a record 11 triple-doubles in a row! Not surprisingly, he had led the league in triple-doubles six times, with a single-season record 42 in 2016–17. And in 2021, he became the league's all-time leader in games with triple-doubles, finishing the 2022 season with 194. As evidence of Westbrook's amazing mix of skills, he also led the NBA in scoring average twice (2015 and 2017). A nine-time All-Star, Westbrook was the 2017 NBA MVP.

FAST FACT: Along with being one of the league's best all-around players, Westbrook regularly wins votes as one of the NBA's best-dressed players.

31.6

WESTBROOK'S HIGHEST
SINGLE-SEASON SCORING AVERAGE,
WHEN HE LED THE LEAGUE
IN 2016–17

Who has made the most free throws in NBA history?

With a tremendous ability to score in the low post and on midrange jumpers, forward **KARL MALONE** was one of the greatest offensive players in NBA history. Malone retired second in career points with 36,928 (he has since been passed by LeBron James). In 19 NBA seasons, Malone shot 13,188 free throws and made 9,787 of them. Both numbers still stand as NBA records.

Malone played in college at Louisiana Tech, where he was nicknamed the Mailman for "delivering" on the court. The Utah Jazz drafted him 13th overall in 1985, teaming him with point guard John Stockton to form one of the greatest duos in NBA history. In 18 seasons together, Stockton ran the pick-and-roll to perfection. Malone averaged 25.4 points per game in that span, finishing in the top five in points per game from 1987–88 through 1999–2000.

Who was the first WNBA player to score 50 points in a game?

Late in the 2013 season, the Tulsa Shock had already been eliminated from playoff contention when they visited the San Antonio Silver Stars. That didn't stop Shock guard **RIQUNA WILLIAMS** from giving it her all in a record-setting performance. In a 98–65 blowout win for Tulsa, Williams scored a WNBA-record 51 points, becoming the first WNBA player to score 50 points in a game. Williams made eight of 14 three-point attempts, went nine-for-nine from the free-throw line, and didn't commit a single turnover in her historic performance.

What WNBA player reached 3,000 points and 1,000 assists fastest?

In a July 3, 2021, game, Phoenix Mercury star guard **SKYLAR DIGGINS-SMITH** passed a unique milestone, cementing her status as one of the WNBA's best all-around players. Diggins-Smith became the first WNBA star to reach 3,000 points, 1,000 assists, and even 200 steals in a career. That she hit milestones in three different areas just shows how much she brings to her team. After a great career at Notre Dame, she was a first-round pick in 2013 by the Tulsa Shock. She has been named to the All-WNBA First Team three times through 2021.

FAST FACT: Though small, Iverson was tough, and rarely came out of games. In fact, he led the NBA in minutes per game seven times.

Who was the second player to lead the NBA in points and steals in the same season?

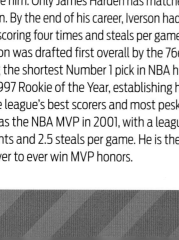

At 6´0˝ tall, Philadelphia 76ers guard **ALLEN IVERSON** was, inch-for-inch, one of the best players in NBA history. Iverson led the league in points and steals per game in the 2000–01 and '01–02 seasons. Only the great Michael Jordan had done that before him. Only James Harden has matched Iverson and Jordan. By the end of his career, Iverson had led the league in scoring four times and steals per game three times.

Iverson was drafted first overall by the 76ers in 1996, becoming the shortest Number 1 pick in NBA history. He was the 1997 Rookie of the Year, establishing himself as one of the league's best scorers and most pesky defenders. Iverson was the NBA MVP in 2001, with a league-leading 31.1 points and 2.5 steals per game. He is the shortest player to ever win MVP honors.

SUPER STAT

10

STEALS MADE BY IVERSON AGAINST THE ORLANDO MAGIC ON MAY 13, 1999, AN NBA PLAYOFF RECORD

Who had the most NBA three-pointers before age 24?

T he NBA has certainly seen a lot of great young players over the years. And since the three-point shot was introduced in 1979, a lot of those youngsters have made their marks from long distance. So it is really saying something that **JAYSON TATUM** of the Boston Celtics set the record for the most treys made before the age of 24. The young star pumped in 764 threes before that birthday came along. He set the new record while leading the NBA in 2021–22 in overall field-goal attempts.

All that shooting success has really paid off for Tatum and the Celtics. Boston chose him third overall in the 2017 NBA Draft and Tatum moved right into the starting lineup. In the four seasons since, he has improved his scoring average each season, while earning three All-Star Game selections. The highlight came in 2022 when he led Boston to the NBA Finals.

SUPER STAT

25.0

PER-GAME SCORING AVERAGE BY TATUM WHEN HE WAS NAMED MVP OF THE EASTERN CONFERENCE FINALS

Who became the first player born outside the United States to lead the NBA in scoring?

As great as Philadelphia 76ers center **JOEL EMBIID** has become, it's a surprise to learn he really didn't play basketball until his early teens. Growing up in Cameroon, he excelled in volleyball. He also played the indoor court sport of handball, which his father has played professionally. Then Embiid saw videotapes of NBA stars like Kobe Bryant and started to dream of a basketball life. He was 6´ 7˝ in junior high, after all! Embiid's parents did not encourage his basketball dreams at first, but came to see it was a way to college and perhaps pro success. Embiid kept growing—reaching his current seven feet—and kept improving, at U.S. high schools and at the University of Kansas. After the Sixers drafted him, he battled foot injuries for two seasons. He has gone on to be one of the best big men in the sport, with five All-Star selections. In 2021–22, he led the NBA with a 30.6 scoring average, the first player born outside the United States to be the scoring champ.

FAST FACT: In 2012–13, Durant became the youngest player to shoot better than 50 percent from the field, 40 percent on three-pointers, and 90 percent on free throws.

SUPER STAT

80

NBA RECORD FOR CONSECUTIVE GAMES OF 25-PLUS POINTS BY WILT CHAMBERLAIN IN 1961–62. DURANT'S BEST WAS 41 IN 2013–14

Who won the scoring title and MVP Award in 2013–14?

klahoma City Thunder forward **KEVIN DURANT** had accomplished more by the age of 25 than most NBA players do in a career. After finishing second in MVP voting to LeBron James two seasons in a row, Durant broke through to win the 2013–14 MVP award. That season he led the NBA in scoring with 32 points per game.

As a freshman at the University of Texas, Durant averaged 25.8 points and 11.1 rebounds in his first and only NCAA season and became the first freshman to be consensus National Player of the Year. The Seattle SuperSonics made Durant the overall Number 2 pick of the 2007 NBA Draft, and he won Rookie of the Year honors in 2007–08. Durant continued to excel as a versatile scorer after the Sonics moved to Oklahoma City and became the Thunder. His 30.1 points per game in 2009–10 gave him his first of four scoring titles. In 2016, he joined the Golden State Warriors and became a champion; he was named the NBA Finals MVP in 2017 and 2018. Durant joined the Brooklyn Nets before the 2020–21 season.

Who scored the most points in a game at Madison Square Garden?

On January 24, 2014, the New York Knicks had lost five straight games leading into a home game against the Charlotte Bobcats. **CARMELO ANTHONY** arrived at Madison Square Garden quieter than usual, but his performance on the court that night was loud and clear: Anthony poured in 62 points, a team record and the most ever scored at the historic Garden. He made 23 of 35 field-goal attempts (good for 65.7 percent) in a 125–96 blowout.

Scoring feats were nothing new for Anthony. In his only college season at Syracuse, he set a Final Four freshman record with a 33-point game against Texas, on his way to earning Most Outstanding Player of the tournament and leading Syracuse to its first national title. Anthony quickly became an NBA star, becoming the second teenager to score 40 points in a game during his rookie year, with the Denver Nuggets. At the 2012 Summer Olympics, he set a Team USA record with 37 points in a win over Nigeria.

Who set the WNBA record for assists in a game?

If there's an assist record in the WNBA, there's a pretty good chance that Chicago's **COURTNEY VANDERSLOOT** holds it. She's the answer to this question thanks to an 18-assist night in a 2020 game. She is also the league's all-time leader in assists-per-game average.

Wait, there's more! Vandersloot led the WNBA in assists in six different seasons during her first 12 years, including 2020 when she had a career-high average of 10.0 assists per game. While leading the Chicago Sky to the 2021 WNBA title, the team's first, she dished out an incredible 102 assists in 10 playoff games. At 5′ 8″, the former Gonzaga star is far from the biggest player on the court, but her vision, ball-handling, and creativity make her one of the most important.

SUPER STAT

300

WNBA SINGLE-SEASON RECORD NUMBER OF ASSISTS COURTNEY VANDERSLOOT DISHED OUT IN 2019

Who was the only player to lead the NCAA, NBA, and ABA in scoring?

Hall of Fame forward **RICK BARRY** had a scoring touch no matter where he played. In 1964–65, he led the nation while playing for the University of Miami, averaging 37.4 points. Then in 1966–67, he led the NBA with 35.6 points per game for the San Francisco Warriors. Barry also scored a league-high 34 points per game for the ABA's Oakland Oaks in 1968–69.

Barry shot free throws in an old-fashioned, underhand style. He made 90 percent of his career NBA foul shots and led the NBA in free-throw shooting six times.

Who once scored eight points in nine seconds in a comeback playoff victory?

In Game 1 of the 1995 Eastern Conference semifinals against the New York Knicks at Madison Square Garden, the Pacers trailed by six points with 18.7 seconds left. Indiana threw an inbounds pass to guard **REGGIE MILLER**, who hit a three-pointer with 16.4 seconds left. Miller then stole the Knicks' inbounds pass, dribbled to get behind the arc, and hit another three to tie the game. After the Knicks missed two foul shots and a follow-up jumper, Miller got the rebound and was fouled. He calmly hit two free throws with 7.5 seconds left to give the Pacers a two-point lead. Knicks guard Greg Anthony fell down as time expired on New York's final possession, giving the Pacers an improbable 107–105 comeback victory.

Who was the youngest player to reach 20,000 career points?

By the time **LeBRON JAMES** was a high school junior, he had already been on the cover of *Sports Illustrated*, was friendly with Michael Jordan, and was a celebrity in northern Ohio. His high school team attracted 4,000 fans per game, and NBA scouts and coaches considered him a surefire superstar. No player had ever received so much hype and attention at such a young age. In 2003, he became the youngest player ever taken first overall in the NBA Draft, the first of many milestones to come.

In 2004, at 19, he became the youngest player to win Rookie of the Year and the youngest to score 40 points in a game. In his second year, he became the youngest All-Star Game MVP. During the 2012–13 season, and shortly after his 28th birthday, James became the youngest player to score 20,000 career points, reaching that mark more than a year younger than any other player in NBA history. Of course, he's done pretty well since then, winning four NBA titles, four NBA MVP awards, and four NBA Finals MVP trophies.

SUPER STAT

2

LeBRON JAMES'S PLACE ON THE NBA ALL-TIME SCORING LIST AFTER HE PASSED KARL MALONE DURING THE 2021–22 SEASON

FAST FACT: Through 2021–22, LeBron James has scored more than 2,000 points in 10 different seasons, one more than Kareem Abdul-Jabbar.

These players were the sparkplugs to their teams' success

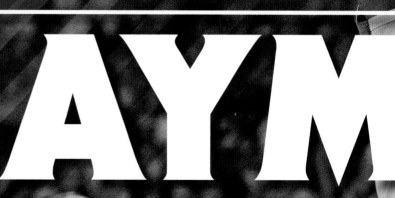

PLAYM

AKERS

Who was the first player to win the Slam Dunk Contest and be named Rookie of the Year in the same season?

He was the Number 1 pick in 2009, but because of a left knee injury, **BLAKE GRIFFIN** of the Los Angeles Clippers didn't make his regular-season debut until 2010. In his first NBA game, he scored 20 points and grabbed 14 rebounds against the Portland Trail Blazers. All season Griffin used his strength and leaping ability to dominate the paint. He finished the season averaging 22.5 points and 12.1 rebounds per game, tops among rookies, and was voted NBA Rookie of the Year.

For all of Griffin's great performances, the most memorable came at All-Star weekend. Competing in the Slam Dunk Contest on his home court, he clinched the title by leaping over a car, catching an alley-oop pass through the sun roof from teammate Baron Davis, and throwing it down.

SUPER STAT

27

CONSECUTIVE DOUBLE-DOUBLES
BY GRIFFIN IN 2010–11, THE
LONGEST ROOKIE STREAK IN
MORE THAN
40 SEASONS

FAST FACT: In high school, Griffin was coached by his father, Tommy Griffin. He won a state title in each of his four seasons.

Which NBA player is depicted on the league's logo?

I n 1969, NBA commissioner J. Walter Kennedy decided the league needed a logo and hired a man named Alan Siegel to create it. Siegel went through hundreds of photos before he landed on the perfect one: Los Angeles Lakers guard **JERRY WEST** dribbling the ball up court. He made a drawing based on the photo—and the NBA had its logo.

Nicknamed Mr. Clutch, West was known for making big plays. He famously hit a 60-foot shot at the buzzer in Game 3 of the 1970 Finals, forcing overtime. The league introduced the NBA Finals MVP award in '69, and even though West's Lakers lost to the Boston Celtics, he still won the award.

After his playing days and a brief stint in coaching, West went on to become a successful general manager for the Lakers and Memphis Grizzlies.

FAST FACT: Parker is a two-time winner of the Wooden award as college basketball's national player of the year.

Who was the first rookie to win WNBA MVP honors?

T he Parkers are a basketball family. Larry Parker played at the University of Iowa. His son Anthony was a longtime pro player for the Toronto Raptors and Cleveland Cavaliers, among other teams. But the family's best basketball career belongs to his daughter, **CANDACE PARKER**, an athletic 6´4″ center who can dunk with ease. As a junior and senior, she led the University of Tennessee to back-to-back NCAA titles, in 2006–07 and '07–08.

The Los Angeles Sparks made Parker the first overall pick of the 2008 WNBA Draft. Teaming with future Hall of Famer Lisa Leslie, she took the Sparks back to the playoffs. Parker averaged 18.5 points, a league-leading 9.5 rebounds, and 2.3 blocks in her first season. Just months after winning an NCAA championship, she was named WNBA MVP, the first rookie to win the award.

Whose 52-point game in 2022 set an NBA Instagram record?

Memphis Grizzlies superstar **JA MORANT** was pretty well-known entering the 2021–22 season. The third-year guard had proven to be one of the NBA's most exciting players, with fearless drives to the hoop and a dazzling array of moves. In 2021–22, however, he and his game took a giant leap forward. As the Grizzlies challenged the Warriors for best record in the West, Morant was the main reason. He ramped up his scoring to a career-high 27.4 points per game, while continuing his dime-dishing work at the point.

On the last day of February, 2022, though, he set a new standard. The NBA's Instagram account posted a series of highlights after Morant poured in a career-best 52 points in a win over the San Antonio Spurs. The league soon announced that with 42 million views to that point, it was the most-viewed clip in NBA history.

SUPER STAT

9.8

NBA-LEADING ASSISTS-PER-GAME AVERAGE FOR MORANT DURING THE 2022 NBA PLAYOFFS

Who has led the league in steals the most times?

To be a great point guard in the NBA, you need to be fast and smart. Point guards are quarterbacks on the court. They not only need to know where their teammates are at any given moment, but also where their opponents are as well.

That's what makes **CHRIS PAUL** one of the best offensive point guards in NBA history. Along with the quickness to blow by defenders, he's great at anticipating how a defense will react to his moves, and how those reactions will lead to points for him or open shots for his teammates.

That high IQ is also what makes Paul one of the best defensive point guards ever to play the game, despite the fact that he's only 6-feet tall.

Paul led the NBA in steals a record six times in his first nine seasons (2005–06 through '13–14). Playing for the New Orleans Hornets, he led the league in steals per game in back-to-back years (2.7 in '07–08 and 2.8 in '08–09), and one more time in '10–11 (2.4 per game). He joined the Los Angeles Clippers the following season, and proceeded to lead the league in steals per game in each of his first three seasons in L.A. Paul joined the Phoenix Suns in 2020 and led the NBA in assists per game with 10.8 in 2021–22.

Who was the first four-time Defensive Player of the Year?

The king of the in-your-face block, **DIKEMBE MUTOMBO**, may have the most famous celebration in the history of the hardwood. But he didn't do it when he scored a basket—he did it when he prevented one.

A 7´2˝ center from the Congo, Mutombo was a prolific shot blocker. Every time he blocked a shot, he celebrated by wagging his index finger as if to say, "No you don't!" Selected fourth overall by the Denver Nuggets in 1991, Mutombo led the league in shot blocking three straight seasons from 1993–94 to '95–96. Mutombo's defensive dominance made the future Hall of Famer the NBA's first four-time Defensive Player of the Year ('94–95, '96–97, '97–98, and 2000–01).

Who was the youngest player ever with a 30-point, 20-rebound triple-double?

Arriving in the NBA in 2018 already a superstar in his native Slovenia, **LUKA DONČIĆ** has more that lived up to the hype. Few players of his size can also show off the lane-driving moves combined with pinpoint outside shooting. Add in Magic Johnson-like creativity as a passer, and you've got one of the NBA's most exciting players. One game in 2020 showed off his complete range of skills. He poured in 34 points as the Dallas Mavericks beat the Sacramento Kings. Dončić also had 20 rebounds and handed out 12 assists. Shy of his 22nd birthday, he became the youngest player ever to have a triple-double of that level.

Dončić and the Mavs had their best season in 2021–22, when he led them in points, assists, and rebounds per game, and made the Western Conference Finals. Look for more from Luka in the future.

Who had the most points ever in their first postseason?

The Phoenix Suns had not been to the NBA playoffs in 11 seasons before putting together an NBA Finals run in the 2020–21 season. A big reason was the ongoing success of then sixth-year shooting guard **DEVIN BOOKER**. (Another was the arrival of superstar Chris Paul to team with Booker.) Booker had grown into a team leader for the Suns, earning his first All-Star Game selection in 2020 and raising his scoring average every year but one to that point.

After finishing with the second-best record in the West, the Suns shined through the playoffs, with Booker being especially hot. He was the top scorer for Phoenix in three of the four rounds of the playoffs, and was the top scorer of five different games. The Suns finally went out in the Final, falling to the Milwaukee Bucks. But when all the points were counted, Booker's 601 points had set an NBA record for a player in his first postseason.

FAST FACT: Nash grew up in Canada, but he was born in Johannesburg, South Africa, where he lived until he was 18 months old.

SUPER STAT

90.4

CAREER FREE-THROW PERCENTAGE FOR NASH, SECOND BEST AMONG PLAYERS WITH AT LEAST 1,200 ATTEMPTS

Who was the first Canadian player to win NBA MVP?

Growing up in Victoria, British Columbia, Canada, **STEVE NASH** didn't play basketball until he was about 12 years old. Nash started his career as an exciting, young point guard for the Phoenix Suns and the Dallas Mavericks, but it wasn't until he returned to Phoenix as a free agent, before the 2004–05 season, that he took his game to the next level.

Surrounded by rising young stars, and directing an exciting, fast-paced offense, Nash averaged a league-leading 11.5 assists per game, made 50.2 percent of his field-goal attempts, and 43.1 percent of his threes. More importantly, with Nash leading the way, the Suns improved by a whopping 33 wins (from 29–53 to 62–20). After missing the playoffs the previous year, Phoenix finished with the best record in the NBA. Nash was named MVP, the first Canadian player to take home that award. A year later, Nash did it again. In 2005–06, he led the league in assists (10.5 per game) and free-throw percentage (92.1), joining Magic Johnson and Stephen Curry as the only point guards to win back-to-back NBA MVP awards.

Who did SI name the "greatest winner in the history of women's basketball"?

No matter where she played, **MAYA MOORE** won. Period. She was the National Player of the Year in high school (twice!), while leading her school to three Georgia state titles. At Connecticut, she twice played on undefeated national-championship teams. That's right—two seasons without losing a game! Moore's all-around game earned her the John Wooden Award in 2009 as the top female player.

Not surprisingly, the Minnesota Lynx made her the top overall pick in the 2011 WNBA Draft . . . and she won Rookie of the Year, of course. In every one of Moore's eight seasons with the Lynx, they had a winning record, including an "odd" list of WNBA title seasons: 2011, 2013, 2015, and 2017. Moore was the WNBA Finals MVP in 2013 and was a three-time winner of the WNBA All-Star Game MVP trophy.

And let's not forget the Olympics. She was on the 2012 and 2016 gold-medal-winning teams that did not lose a single contest in those two Games. Add it all up and Moore won 85 percent of the basketball games she played in. She's off to win in another way, retiring to focus on ministry and social justice.

SUPER STAT

4

NUMBER OF WNBA CAREER KEY STAT TOP 10s FOR TAMIKA CATCHINGS: POINTS, TOTAL REBOUNDS, STEALS, AND ASSISTS

Who won the most WNBA Defensive Player of the Year Awards?

Hall of famer **TAMIKA CATCHINGS** was finishing a great career at the University of Tennessee when she tore the ACL in her right knee. Even though she had to sit out for an entire season, the Indiana Fever still selected her third overall in that year's draft. It was a risk, but it paid off.

Catchings was the league's Rookie of the Year and an All-Star in 2002. She made the All-Star team nine times through 2014. She also won the WNBA MVP award in 2011 and led the Fever to a title in 2012.

Catchings is not just a great offensive player. She has won five Defensive Player of the Year Awards, more than any player in league history. She has also led the WNBA in steals per game seven times and is the all-time leader in career steals (1,074).

Archibald was inducted into the Basketball Hall of Fame in 1991.

Who is the youngest WNBA player to record a triple-double?

In 2021, **SABRINA IONESCU** of the New York Liberty wasted little time making her mark on the WNBA. In only her sixth game, she had 26 points, 12 assists, and 10 rebounds, making her—at 23—the youngest ever with a tripl-double in the league. She became the youngest with two such games when she repeated her feat during the 2022 season. Only nine other WNBA players had any triple-doubles in their careers, and Ionescu already had three by season three!

This kind of multi-stat success is nothing new for Ionescu. In college at Oregon, she racked up 26 triple-double games. That is not only almost three times as many as any other female college player, it's twice as many as any male college player! Not surprisingly, she was a three-time All-American and a two-time player of the year award winner.

Who was the only player to lead the NBA in scoring and assists in the same season?

Point guards usually fall into one of two categories: scorers who pile up points or playmakers who set up their teammates. In 1972–73, Kansas City-Omaha Kings point guard **NATE (TINY) ARCHIBALD** filled both roles, and did something no player had done before or since.

Archibald tore up opposing defenses, averaging an NBA-leading 34.0 points per game. But he didn't forget about his teammates. Archibald handed out a remarkable 11.4 assists per game, also tops in the league. He's the only player to ever lead the NBA in both of those categories in the same season. Archibald later won an NBA title with the Boston Celtics in 1980–81.

SUPER STAT

4

TIMES GARNETT WAS NBA PLAYER OF THE MONTH IN 2003–04, THE FIRST TIME A PLAYER HAD WON THE AWARD FOUR TIMES IN ONE SEASON

Who was the last player to lead the league in rebounding four straight seasons?

The Minnesota Timberwolves took a big chance on draft night in 1995. The franchise had never won 30 games in a season, let alone competed for a playoff spot. It needed a star. And it found one in a high school player from Chicago named **KEVIN GARNETT**.

It wasn't long before Garnett brought respectability to the T-Wolves. In just his second season, he lifted them to the playoffs for the first time. He was big (6´11˝) and a skilled athlete who was a force on defense. His intensity allowed him to become one of the greatest players ever on that end of the court. Garnett led the NBA in rebounding four straight seasons, from 2003–04 (when he was the league's MVP) through '06–07. He is the last player to win the rebounding crown in four consecutive seasons.

Despite some great years, the Timberwolves could never break through in the tough Western Conference. Garnett was traded to the Boston Celtics before '07–08 and helped the Celtics win an NBA championship. He wrapped up his Hall of Fame career with two seasons back in Minnesota, retiring in 2016.

FAST FACT: Rose won two Illinois high school titles at Simeon Career Academy in Chicago.

Who was the youngest player to win the NBA MVP award?

Before the 2010–11 season started, young Chicago Bulls point guard **DERRICK ROSE** had a question for the basketball world: "Why can't I be the MVP of the league?" The obvious answer was that Rose was only 22 years old. No one had ever won the NBA's MVP award before the age of 23 (and that was more than 40 years ago, when **WES UNSELD** of the Baltimore Bullets won the award in 1968–69).

But Rose took his game to a new level in his third NBA season. He was already one of the most explosive guards in the league when it came to attacking the basket, and he was a smart point guard who made his teammates better. That year, he added a greatly improved jump shot, averaging a career-high 25 points to go along with 7.7 assists per game. More importantly, he made the Bulls a title contender. With an improved Rose leading the way, they finished with an NBA-best record of 62–20.

Rose answered his own question and beat out Orlando's Dwight Howard, Miami's LeBron James, Kobe Bryant of the Los Angeles Lakers, and Oklahoma City's Kevin Durant to become the youngest ever to take home league MVP.

Who was the first player in NBA history with 2,000 points, 1,000 rebounds, and 500 assists in a season?

Some players can fill the basket with points. Others can clean the glass. Still others dish out perfect pass after perfect pass. Then there are players like **NIKOLA JOKIĆ**, the Denver Nuggets' two-time NBA MVP. Actually, there are not really a lot of other players like the big man from Serbia. After joining the Nuggets in 2015, he took a couple of seasons to adjust to NBA play. But he came with great ball skills, an inside game, and the kind of shooting touch rarely seen in a player who stands 6′11″. He put it all together in the 2020–21 season and won his first MVP. In 2022, he started hot and stayed hotter. In a game in April, he became the first player in NBA history with 2,000 points, 1,000 rebounds, and 500 assists in the same season. Reaching the milestone took a little extra grit from Jokić. An elbow from an opponent opened a cut on his head that had to be bandaged several times. But when the Nuggets walked off winners, the real reward for Jokić and his teammates was that they clinched another playoff berth.

SUPER STAT

2016

THE YEAR THAT JOKIĆ HELPED SERBIA WIN THE OLYMPIC SILVER MEDAL, FINISHING SECOND TO THE UNITED STATES

Who was the first NBA player to have a season with 1,000 points, 500 rebounds and assists, and 100 steals and blocks?

Golden State Warriors forward **DRAYMOND GREEN** is like a human Swiss Army knife. He's not the very best at any one thing on the basketball court, but he's very good at a little bit of everything. In 2015–16, he showed off that hoops versatility when he became the first player to top each of these stat milestones: 1,000 points, 500 rebounds, 500 assists, 100 blocks, and 100 steals.

Green was a second-round pick and was more of a role player for his first two seasons. But he soon connected with Stephen Curry and Klay Thompson to form the backbone of what would become one of the NBA's dominant dynasties. While the "Splash Brothers" and Kevin Durant (for three seasons) piled up points, Green did the hard work on defense and on the glass. With his help, the Warriors have four NBA titles.

FAST FACT: Green was named the NBA Defensive Player of the Year for the 2016–17 season, one of the Warriors' championship campaigns.

Who was the first player to average 23 points on 60 percent shooting in his first 50 games?

The city of New Orleans and all of its Pelicans fans got some great news in the summer of 2022. After missing an entire NBA season with a foot injury, **ZION WILLIAMSON** was cleared to return at full speed. Pelicans fans hope he is able to pick up where he left off.

Williamson was a high-flying, slam-dunking phenom in high school in South Carolina. Not only did he lead his team to three state titles, he won national dunk contests, and regularly appeared in the top ranks of recruits. At Duke, even though he missed games with a foot injury, he was the ACC Player of the Year and a regular on highlight shows for his aerial ability.

The Pelicans made him the first overall pick but a knee injury kept him from debuting until January 2020. Still only 19, he made up for lost time. He scored at least 20 points in 19 of his 24 games that season, some on rim-rattling dunks. He opened the 2020–21 season hot as well. By the 50th game of his career, he was averaging 23 points a game while shooting 60 percent, something no other NBA player had done.

FAST FACT: As a college player in 2019, Williamson hurt his foot when his Nike sneaker broke open during a game. The value of Nike stock fell overnight!

SUPER STAT

36

POINTS WILLIAMSON SCORED IN A 2021 GAME WHILE SHOOTING 90 PERCENT, MAKING HIM THE YOUNGEST PLAYER TO DO SO

PLAYER INDEX

PHOTO CREDITS

Cover: Illustration by MMJ Studio/AA Reps Inc.
Front Cover: Kohjiro Kinno for Sports Illustrated (Sue Bird); Manny Millan for Sports Illustrated (Michael Jordan); Greg Nelson for Sports Illustrated (Stephen Curry)
Back Cover: John W. McDonough for Sports Illustrated (LeBron James); AP Photo/Brandon Dill (Ja Morant); Erick W. Rasco for Sports Illustrated (Jayson Tatum); Kohjiro Kinno for Sports Illustrated Classic (A'Ja Wilson)
Page 3: Erick W. Rasco for Sports Illustrated (Sue Bird); David E. Klutho for Sports Illustrated (Anthony Davis); John W. McDonough for Sports Illustrated (Dirk Nowitzki); Greg Nelson for Sports Illustrated (Kevin Durant); AP Photo/Brandon Dill (Ja Morant)
Pages 4-5: Manny Millan for Sports Illustrated (Hakeem Olajuwon); John W. McDonough for Sports Illustrated (Shaquille O'Neal); Andy Hayt for Sports Illustrated (Larry Bird); AP Photo/ Phelan M. Ebenhack (Breanna Stewart)
Pages 6-7: John W. McDonough for Sports Illustrated
Pages 8-9: AP Photo/David J. Phillip (Cynthia Cooper); Neil Leifer for Sports Illustrated (Bill Russell); David E. Klutho for Sports Illustrated (LeBron James)
Pages 10-11: John W. McDonough for Sports Illustrated
Pages 12-13: AP Photo/Roy Dabner (Lauren Jackson); John W. McDonough for Sports Illustrated (Kawhi Leonard)
Pages 14-15: John W. McDonough for Sports Illustrated
Pages 16-17: Icon Sportswire via AP Images (Isiah Thomas); AP Photo/Charles Knoblock (George Mikan); Andy Hayt for Sports Illustrated (Larry Bird)
Pages 18-19: AP Photo/Paul Beaty
Pages 20-21: Manny Millan for Sports Illustrated (Hakeem Olajuwon); AP Photo/Reed Saxon (James Worthy); AP Photo/Phelan M. Ebenhack (Breanna Stewart)
Pages 22-23: Manny Millan for Sports Illustrated (Michael Jordan)
Pages 24-25: Erick W. Rasco for Sports Illustrated (Sue Bird); AP Photo/Marcio Jose Sanchez (Kevin Durant)
Pages 26-27: Greg Nelson for Sports Illustrated
Pages 28-29: Neil Leifer for Sports Illustrated (Julius Erving); David E. Klutho for Sports Illustrated (James Harden, Anthony Davis); Ethan Miller/Getty Images (Becky Hammon)
Pages 30-31: David E. Klutho for Sports Illustrated
Pages 32-33: Andy Hayt for Sports Illustrated (George Gervin); Al Tielemans for Sports Illustrated (Pau Gasol, Marc Gasol); Manny Millan for Sports Illustrated (Muggsy Bogues)

Pages 34-35: AP Photo/Roberto Borea (Gheorghe Muresan); Neil Leifer for Sports Illustrated (Julius Erving)
Pages 36-37: AP Photo/Elaine Thompson
Pages 38-39: Andy Hayt for Sports Illustrated (Earvin Johnson); Kohjiro Kinno for Sports Illustrated (A'Ja Wilson); David E. Klutho for Sports Illustrated (Sylvia Fowles)
Pages 40-41: Greg Nelson for Sports Illustrated
Pages 42-43: Bob Rosato for Sports Illustrated
Pages 44-45: John W. McDonough for Sports Illustrated (Vince Carter); Ethan Miller/Getty Images (Becky Hammon); Manny Millan for Sports Illustrated (Manute Bol)
Pages 46-47: AP Photo/Morry Gash
Pages 48-49: Icon Sportswire via AP Images (Dominique Wilkins); Cal Sport Media via AP Images (Nneka Ogwumike and Chiney Ogwumike); David E. Klutho for Sports Illustrated (Rudy Gobert)
Pages 50-51: David E. Klutho for Sports Illustrated
Pages 52-53: Bill Frakes for Sports Illustrated (Kyrie Irving); Manny Millan for Sports Illustrated (Charles Barkley)
Pages 54-55: Greg Nelson for Sports Illustrated (Anthony Edwards); Manny Millan for Sports Illustrated (Dennis Rodman); John W. McDonough for Sports Illustrated (Dirk Nowitzki); Rich von Biberstein/Icon Sportswire via AP Images (Diana Taurasi)
Pages 56-57: Greg Nelson for Sports Illustrated
Pages 58-59: Manny Millan for Sports Illustrated (Robert Parish); Jeffrey Brown/Icon Sportswire via AP Images (Liz Cambage); AP Photo/Ben Margot (Klay Thompson)
Pages 60-61: AP Photo/Matt York
Pages 62-63: AP Photo/Al Messerschmidt (Scott Skiles); Manny Millan for Sports Illustrated (Kareem Abdul-Jabbar)
Pages 64-65: Manny Millan for Sports Illustrated
Pages 66-67: Bettmann/Getty Images (Oscar Robertson); AP Photo/Douglas C. Pizac (Mark Eaton); Kohjiro Kinno for Sports Illustrated (Elena Delle Donne)
Pages 68-69: John W. McDonough for Sports Illustrated
Pages 70-71: John W. McDonough for Sports Illustrated (Dirk Nowitzki); AP Photo/Tim Sharp (A.C. Green)
Pages 72-73: Manny Millan for Sports Illustrated
Pages 74-75: Manny Millan for Sports Illustrated (Scottie Pippen); Greg Nelson for Sports Illustrated (Anthony Edwards); Greg Nelson for Sports Illustrated (Donovan Mitchell)
Pages 76-77: Rich von Biberstein/Icon Sportswire via AP Images
Pages 78-79: Timothy A. Clary/AFP via Getty Images

Pages 80-81: Greg Nelson for Sports Illustrated (Kevin Durant, Russell Westbrook); AP Photo/Bill Kostroun (Carmelo Anthony); David E. Klutho for Sports Illustrated (Riquna Williams)
Pages 82-83: John W. McDonough for Sports Illustrated
Pages 84-85: Neil Leifer for Sports Illustrated (Wilt Chamberlain); Erick W. Rasco for Sports Illustrated (Tina Charles); Manny Millan for Sports Illustrated (Steve Kerr)
Pages 86-87: Greg Nelson for Sports Illustrated
Pages 88-89: AP Photo/Al Messerschmidt (Karl Malone); AP Photo/Rick Scuteri (Skylar Diggins-Smith); David E. Klutho for Sports Illustrated (Riquna Williams)
Pages 90-91: Manny Millan for Sports Illustrated
Pages 92-93: Erick W. Rasco for Sports Illustrated (Jayson Tatum); Greg Nelson for Sports Illustrated (Joel Embiid)
Pages 94-95: Greg Nelson for Sports Illustrated
Pages 96-97: AP Photo/Bill Kostroun
Pages 98-99: Erick W. Rasco for Sports Illustrated (Courtney Vandersloot); Manny Millan for Sports Illustrated (Reggie Miller); Neil Leifer for Sports Illustrated (Rick Barry)
Pages 100-101: John W. McDonough for Sports Illustrated
Pages 102-103: John W. McDonough for Sports Illustrated (Luka Dončić); David E. Klutho for Sports Illustrated (Maya Moore); AP Photo/ Brandon Dill (Ja Morant); Ezra Shaw/Getty Images (Nikola Jokić)
Pages 104-105: Robert Beck for Sports Illustrated
Pages 106-107: AP Photo (Jerry West); Peter Read Miller for Sports Illustrated (Candace Parker); AP Photo/Brandon Dill (Ja Morant)
Pages 108-109: Christian Petersen/Getty Images
Pages 110-111: John Biever for Sports Illustrated (Dikembe Mutombo); Greg Nelson for Sports Illustrated (Devin Booker); John W. McDonough for Sports Illustrated (Luka Dončić)
Pages 112-113: John W. McDonough for Sports Illustrated
Pages 114-115: David E. Klutho for Sports Illustrated
Pages 116-117: Jeffrey Brown/Icon Sportswire via AP Images (Tamika Catchings); Neil Leifer for Sports Illustrated (Nate Archibald); Erick W. Rasco for Sports Illustrated (Sabrina Ionescu)
Pages 118-119: Bob Rosato for Sports Illustrated
Pages 120-121: David E. Klutho for Sports Illustrated
Pages 122-123: Ezra Shaw/Getty Images (Nikola Jokić); AP Photo/Rich Pedroncelli (Draymond Green)
Pages 124-125: Greg Nelson for Sports Illustrated